Madeira

Front cover: view over Funchal harbour

Right: man in traditional headgear

TOP 10 ATTRACTIONS

The Adegas de São Francisco · Visit the oldest working wine lodge in Madeira *(pages 27–8)*

Madeira's hills and mountains ·
Venture out on spectacular scenic walks *(page 55)*

Monte · The fashionable hilltop town above Funchal is best known for its exhilarating toboggan rides *(page 39)*

Jardim Botânico · Marvel at Madeira's extravagant flowers *(page 36–7)*

Pico do Arieiro
Drive above the clouds to the top of Madeira's second-highest peak *(page 54)*

Madeira's lido complexes
Enjoy a dip *(page 86)*

São Vicente One of Madeira's most attractive villages, with volcanic caves nearby *(page 50)*

Funchal's Museu de Arte Sacra Outstanding Flemish paintings enjoy pride of place in this museum *(page 30)*

Palheiro cottages These traditional thatched cottages are still in use in the Santana region *(page 57)*

Porto Santo Relax on gorgeous golden sands on this nearby island *(page 64)*

CONTENTS

45

21

82

13

48

88

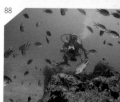

INTRODUCTION

A mere speck in the middle of the Atlantic Ocean, Madeira is a volcanic island thickly draped with vegetation, a colourful riot of flowers and fruit trees. Rugged mountains peek through the clouds, and microclimates hover over isolated villages. Spectacular cliffs crash down to the surf below.

Although the islands were known to Roman and Carthaginian sailors 2,000 years ago, Madeira was first settled only a few decades before Columbus made his way to America. It became part of the Portuguese empire after the great expedition teams of the 15th century claimed it for King João I. But Madeira is nearer to Africa than to Lisbon. It lies 600km (375 miles) off the coast of Morocco and nearly 1,000km (600 miles) southwest of the Portuguese capital.

Formed from volcanic eruptions many millions of years ago, Madeira is an archipelago. The land is like an iceberg; massive mountains poke through the clouds, forming the mere tip of a submerged mass. Apart from Madeira itself, only one other island in the group is inhabited – the arid, much flatter holiday hideaway of Porto Santo. Christopher Columbus visited Porto Santo in the second half of the 15th century, and married the local governor's granddaughter.

Natural Wonders

Few places on earth can rival Madeira's wealth of natural gifts, especially in so small an area. The island is blanketed with flowers: birds of paradise display their bright orange, beak-like flowers in open fields. Fragrant hydrangeas line walking paths skirting the edges of mountain terraces. Private and public gardens burst with orchids, bougainvillea

Historic Funchal viewed from Pico dos Barcelos

and jacarandas trees, while orchards and plantations heave with apples, pears, cherries, passion fruit, bananas and avocados.

In the mountains, water streams down from unseen springs: a one-hour walk might take you past half a dozen waterfalls. The cold waters around the island, once prime whaling territory, are now a marine sanctuary for whales, dolphins and seals. And all of this in year-round sub-tropical weather with a southerly breeze and temperatures that average 22°C (72°F) in the summer and 17°C (63°F) during the winter.

Madeira is renowned for its spectacular exotic blooms

Size and Population

Madeira seems much larger than its diminutive size, just 57km (35 miles) long and 22km (13 miles) wide. The terrain is so mountainous, and its roads so tortuous, that distances are magnified in terms of both time and effort. This can breed insularity; until fast roads were constructed in the decade since 1997, some villagers never travelled to the capital, Funchal, let alone to mainland Portugal. Yet young and upwardly mobile islanders do go off in search of fortune, and the most successful return from overseas to build sumptuous villas.

Madeira, alas, is no simple portrait of a Gauguin-like tropical paradise. With a history of emigration and return, of welcoming visiting merchants and, during a brief period of occupation, a garrison of British troops, islanders are a cosmopolitan mix. The populace is a stew of dark North African complexions and blonde, blue-eyed northern Europeans.

The Capital City

Funchal, the island's capital, major harbour and only city of any note, merely hints at Madeira's riches. The capital's white houses with tile roofs are clustered on picturesque hills sloping

Desertas and Selvagens

As well as the two inhabited islands of Madeira and Porto Santo, the archipelago comprises another five islands and numerous minor rocks and reefs, all situated in the North Atlantic Ocean. The islands fall into two groups: the Ilhas Desertas (desert islands) and Ilhas Selvagens (wild or savage islands).

The former consist of three islands, the nearest situated 12km (19 miles) southeast of Madeira. These desert islands are far from the Robinson Crusoe idyll: they are barren and inhospitable to the point where, aside from the occasional goat and rabbit, the most notable land creature is a large, poisonous black spider.

But the sea life around the islands is a different story. Dolphins and turtles are occasionally spotted, and there is a colony of very rare monk seals. Birdwatchers will relish the opportunity to see shearwaters and petrels. Marine biologists and nature conservationists are the only regular human visitors, for even though excursion boats frequently make trips to these isles in summer, landing is restricted to authorised persons only.

Meanwhile, the two Selvagens Islands, usually known as Grande (large) and Pequena (small), are Madeiran only in name. They lie 285km (177 miles) to the south and are actually closer to the Canary Islands than to Madeira. Like the Desertas, they are uninhabited and devoted entirely to nature conservation.

Funchal is a major harbour

down to a steep bay, which makes for a pretty picture. The city is undeniably pleasant, but there are parts of town where the noise and traffic don't seem so far removed from the places most people come here to avoid.

Almost half of Madeira's 270,000 people live in Funchal (pronounced 'foon-shawl'), and passengers from cruise ships stride ashore daily for a frenzied flurry of sightseeing and shopping. Other visitors chill out in luxury hotels crowding the city's western clifftops. In recent years a gleaming new high-rise *zona turista* has sprung up to confront the old-world hotels and distinguished *quintas* (rural estates) of Madeira's more peaceful past.

The Rural Interior

Funchal is less the sum of Madeira, though, than a gateway to the rest of the island, whose real charms begin in the hillsides just a few minutes outside the town. Spectacular gardens, including the Botanic Garden and Quinta do Palheiro, are only a short bus, taxi or cable-car ride from the capital.

Small-scale agriculture dominates the island's landscape, and employs about a fifth of its people. Depending on the altitude,

Isolated villages

Some of the mountain villages of Madeira are so isolated that they did not begin to receive TV signals until the 1980s.

and whether you happen to be on the warm south coast or the marginally cooler north coast, you will see terraces of bananas and vines that produce the grapes for fortified Madeira wine. There are windswept mountain peaks, craggy cliffs and emerald valleys. From strategically situated lookout points *(miradouros)* you can take in these magical panoramas and look down upon villages and terraced fields carved out of the mountains.

New roads and tunnels make driving around Madeira faster than before, though the best scenery is reserved for those who follow the hairpin bends of mountain roads and coastal lanes, getting sprayed by waterfalls and constantly stopping to enjoy spectacular vistas. Madeira is even better when explored on two feet. The island is heaven for anyone who enjoys being outside, whether your taste runs to gentle walks or hardcore hiking. Madeira's system of irrigation channels, known as *levadas*,
carries water down from the mountains on gentle gradients and provides a ready-made system of trails. The canals – more than 2,100km (1,300 miles) of them wrap around the island – have level footpaths running along their entire length. Walkers of all ages and abilities need only find a *levada* to take in some of the finest countryside anywhere. Several of these walks, which are described later in this book *(see pages 84–5)*, are among the highlights of Madeira.

With such rapturous scenery and a climate that is consistently delightful, perhaps it would be unfair to

Agriculture on a small scale

expect nature to have bestowed the island with miles of perfect sands as well. Madeira has few beaches as such – although most coastal villages have swimming pools and sea access, and Calheta has an artificial beach. But if a chair by the pool just can't compare with waves lapping on sand, you'll have to follow in the wake of Columbus and dock on the neighbouring island of Porto Santo, a popular day trip. The only other inhabited island in the archipelago, Porto Santo has a 9-km (5½-mile) beach running the length of its south coast, but few other attractions.

While some surely would find the notion of an island holiday with no beach time an unusual prospect indeed, perhaps it isn't at all a tragedy that Madeira's shoreline crashes so violently into the ocean. A Madeira with sandy beaches and cheap flights from Europe and North America would surely not have been capable of staving off the mass-tourist market as it has thus far. Lack of sand has kept Madeira from becoming as popular as the Canary Islands or Mallorca.

Tourism and Madeira

For decades, Madeira has instead attracted a genteel, even anachronistic, form of island tourism. Afternoon tea and black-tie dinners are still served at the most elegant hotels. The typical visitor is still older and wealthier than in most holiday destinations, but times are beginning to change – as they are across Portugal, no longer the forgotten backwater of Europe. Funchal's enlarged airport and many new hotels testify to local travel industry ambitions. Today Madeira is being discovered by younger travellers who might also indulge in the spas and dining that world-class hotels offer, but are just as likely to seek out the modest inns up in the mountains and strap on their boots for serious hiking.

Madeirans, like most Portuguese, are a generally quiet and reserved people. Add to this geographical isolation and the

Ponta de São Lourenço, Madeira's easternmost point

difficulties for most of a harsh agricultural existence (where few have the machinery to help cultivate the tiny terraced fields) and you might well forgive the islanders if they seemed less than welcoming. Instead, you will find friendly people who, in spite of a 12-month season that for decades has deposited tourists from wealthier nations on their shores, are refreshingly hospitable. They are proud of the scenic beauty, delectable wines and exquisite hand embroidery for which their tiny island has rightly become famous.

The tourism ante is being upped by hoteliers, entrepreneurs and government officials eager to broaden Madeira's offerings and appeal. However, the allure of Madeira remains its absence of man-made attractions and its abundance of natural ones. Some people still suggest that Madeira is part of the lost continent of Atlantis, and, although it has become progressively easier to get there, the island still seems other-worldly.

A BRIEF HISTORY

As befits a lush, tropical island stranded in the middle of the ocean, Madeira's origins are shrouded in fanciful legend. Some claim that the archipelago is what remains of Plato's lost Atlantis, or part of a landmass that once fused the continents of Europe and America. Recorded history of the archipelago begins in relatively recent times: in the early 15th century, just as the golden age of Portuguese discovery was erupting. Under the direction of Henry the Navigator, caravels set out from the westernmost point of the Algarve, in southern Portugal, in search of foreign lands, fame and

The First Man on Madeira?

Some say that the first man to set foot on the island was not the Portuguese adventurer João Gonçalves Zarco but a 14th-century Englishman named Robert Machim (sometimes written Machin).

One version of the story is that Machim was a knight at the court of Edward III and sought to marry above his class, to a girl named Anne d'Arfet (or Anne of Hertford). The determined young lovers boarded a France-bound ship, which was thrown severely off-course. The pair ended up shipwrecked on Madeira. Anne died of exposure soon afterwards, and Machim buried her by the bay where they had come ashore. Machim too died (it is said of a broken heart) and was buried alongside her by members of the same shipwrecked crew, who eventually escaped on a log raft and lived to recount the tragic tale.

Zarco, who is much more widely credited with the discovery of Madeira, was aware of the legend. He is said to have found the grave of the couple, naming the site Machico in honour of Machim. The couple's resting place is said to be beneath the Capela dos Milagres on the eastern side of Machico Bay (see page 61).

wealth. João Gonçalves Zarco, sailing in the service of Prince Henry, made the first of many famous Portuguese discoveries: in 1418 he happened upon a small volcanic archipelago 1,000km (600 miles) from Lisbon.

Perhaps Zarco knew precisely where he was heading, having learned of the existence of Madeira from a Castilian source. After all, the waters of the Canary Islands, only 445km (275 miles) to the south, had lain in busy shipping lanes for very nearly a century, and Genovese maps from the mid-14th century depict both Madeira and Porto Santo.

More likely, Zarco was heading for Guinea and storms forced him on to the beach of Porto Santo. If so, then he was fortunate, for he managed to land on the only large, sandy beach for hundreds of miles around.

Portugal's First Colony

The following year Zarco returned to claim the larger island he had seen from Porto Santo, and with him went Tristão Vaz Teixeira and Bartolomeu Perestrelo. They officially became the first men to set foot on the heavily forested island, naming it *Ilha da Madeira*, 'Island of Timber'.

The Portuguese Crown, delighted with its first important discovery, immediately embarked on a programme of colonisation. In 1425, King João I pronounced Madeira an official province of Portugal, and presented it as a gift to Prince Henry. He, in turn, confirmed the land ownership rights to Zarco and Teixeira, while Perestrelo was awarded Porto Santo.

Henry the Navigator

Occupation of Madeira began in the early 1420s as a decidedly small-scale project: colonists arrived with only as much as they could carry from Portugal. They found plenty of water pouring down from the mountains, and more timber than anyone knew what to do with. So they set about clearing the land for agriculture, setting fire to massive tracts of forest. Legend says that a great fire burned for seven years on the island.

Energetic Agriculture

The fire provided the soil with a rich ash fertiliser, which complemented the luxuriant growing conditions of tropical sun and plentiful water. The Portuguese saw valuable economic opportunity in their new possession and sent for Malvasia grapes from Crete and sugar-cane from Sicily in an effort to seed the island's first cash crops. The project was not a simple one. Colonists had to find enough level ground to grow crops on, and then solve the issue of irrigating them. Brute strength, without the aid of machinery, carved flat surfaces out of the mountains, and settlers built the terraces that are seen today on the steep slopes.

Columbus arrived as a sugar-trader and became a resident

CRISTOVÃO COLOMBO

The problem of watering crops was solved by the irrigation system known as *levadas* – simply designed water channels that wound down from water sources on the verdant mountain tops. The *levadas* were largely built by slave labourers from Africa, whose primary employment was on sugar plantations. Madeirans traded sugar, the era's dominant luxury item, with Venice and Flanders, and they proved skilful in the art of wine-

First inhabitants

It seems certain that Madeira had never been inhabited before the Portuguese arrived in the 15th century. The first settlers found no Stone Age natives, as the Spanish had found on the Canary Islands, and no mysterious monuments to the past, as on the Balearics.

making. The island's burgeoning economic significance propelled population growth, and by the middle of the 15th century Madeira was home to 800 families. A 1514 census recorded 5,000 inhabitants (not including slaves).

In 1478 Madeira welcomed a visitor who would greatly assist the island's future wine trade. Christopher Columbus, not yet a sailor of any renown, sailed to Madeira on an assignment to buy sugar-cane. His sojourn was unsuccessful, as money failed to arrive for part of the shipment. Yet Columbus (Cristóvão Colombo in Portuguese) returned six years later, by which time evidence suggests that he had become an experienced sugar-cane merchant. His later discovery of the New World brought prosperity to the Madeiran economy: the island's strategic location on the great East–West trading route meant that ships anchored and took on food, water and the valuable trading commodity of Madeira wine.

Columbus married Dona Filipa Moniz Perestrelo, the granddaughter of Porto Santo's first governor, and fathered a son on the island. Even today, there are those on Porto Santo who will tell you that it was during the time he spent there that Columbus learned navigation techniques, and found the inspiration to undertake his voyage of 1492.

Plundered by Pirates

From early in the 16th century, Madeira became the target of pirate attacks. Noticing the island's burgeoning wealth and repository of supplies, buccaneers from Morocco, Algeria and France invaded coastal settlements, plundered villages and left behind them a trail of death and destruction. In 1566 Madeira suffered its worst disaster when the French pirate Bertrand de Montluc sailed into Funchal harbour with his 11-galleon armada and 1,300 men. He unleashed a 16-day reign of terror that left 300 Madeirans dead, stocks of sugar destroyed and the island plundered. By the time Lisbon mounted a rescue mission, the pirates had long fled.

As a result of the attack, Porto Santo, which had also been scourged by these villains of the seas, went on to build hilltop beacons to serve as early-warning systems, which allowed the citizens to defend themselves or flee if necessary.

Looe Rock and Funchal in the early 19th century

On the mainland, an invasion of even greater significance ensued in 1580, when Philip II of Spain proclaimed himself king of Portugal and marched his armies across the border. The Spanish remained for another 60 years, during which time Madeira was a Spanish territory.

At the end of the 16th century, Madeira surrendered its domination of the

Pirate treasure

The notorious English pirate Captain Kidd was was hanged in London after terrorising the high seas for almost 10 years – but the loot he amassed was never found. Legend has it that his treasure is buried somewhere on the Ilhas Desertas, southeast of Madeira, although all searches so far have found nothing.

sugar-cane industry to another, much larger, Portuguese colony: Brazil. Sugar-cane had taken a hefty toll on the Madeiran soil; the exhausted plantation soils were supplanted by less demanding grape vines. Although sugar-cane is still grown today (for molasses and the brandy-like *aguardente*), it has long ceased to be Madeira's major crop.

Madeira and Britain

Britain's political and economic connections to Madeira can be traced to the 17th century. In 1662 Charles II married Portugal's Catherine of Bragança, and a provision written into the bride's dowry granted special favours to British settlers on Madeira. Both Madeira and Britain benefited from a new regulation that governed the shipment of Madeira wine and made it the only wine that could be exported directly to the British possessions in the Western hemisphere (all other wines had to be shipped to the Americas via a British harbour). Such trading rights attracted more Britons to the island, who founded dynastic families which, in some cases, still constitute the island's economic elite. Wine profits were huge, and by 1800 exports had reached nine million bottles per year. Many of the grand country *quintas* (villas) that still dot the island today have their roots in the early Madeira wine industry.

British troops arrived on the island in 1801 to protect against possible invasion by the French, but they were withdrawn following the Treaty of Amiens in 1802. In 1807 the treaty was put in jeopardy and the troops returned, remaining until 1814. After the fall of Napoleon, many of the garrison remained and settled permanently on the island.

The second half of the 19th century on Madeira was plagued by natural disaster. In 1852 the island's precious vines were blighted by mildew, wiping out an estimated 90 percent of the total crop. Just four years later, cholera claimed the lives of up to 7,000 Madeirans, and in 1872–3 the dreaded phylloxera louse destroyed the remainder of the vineyards. Potato and sugar crops were also badly affected.

Portugal took up arms during World War I, siding with the British and French. Madeira's strategic position for Atlantic shipping did not escape the notice of the German

Celebrated Stopovers

Madeira has welcomed many distinguished sea voyagers in its long tradition of hospitality, including, in 1815, the defeated Napoleon Bonaparte. En route to exile on St Helena in the South Atlantic, Napoleon's ship anchored to take on supplies. The only visitor allowed aboard was the British consul, who graciously presented Britain's old enemy with bottles of vintage Madeira wine to help wile away his confinement. (Napoleon responded with gold coins.)

History just about repeated itself after the 1974 coup, when the deposed Portuguese leaders, ex-President Tomás and Prime Minister Caetano, also stopped at Madeira en route to exile in Brazil. This time, however, the defeated party was allowed ashore – but only to be locked up in the São Lourenço fortress.

An *azulejo* frieze depicting a British tourist being carried by local men adorns Funchal's former Chamber of Commerce

High Command, and in 1916 a German submarine bombarded Funchal harbour and sank three French ships.

Modern Times

As mainland Portugal lurched into a political and economic crisis that would bring down the country's republican government, many miles away Madeira was busy developing its tourist trade: the island had been a sought-after destination since the mid-19th century, attracting wealthy British sunlovers, minor royalty and aristocrats from many countries. The celebrated Reid's Hotel had opened its doors in 1890, and a seaplane service started operating from Southampton in 1921. Madeira was awarded further cachet when the last of the Austro-Hungarian emperors, Charles I of Austria (also Charles IV of Hungary), chose Madeira as his home in exile after World War I. He died here in 1922 and his last resting

Madeira appeals to tourists in a 1931 poster

place, in Monte's Nossa Senhora church, now receives a stream of pilgrims following his beatification by Pope John Paul II.

In 1932 Portugal gained a new ruler, Dr António Salazar. His success at controlling inflation and reducing national debt made him a popular hero, but under the new ultra-conservative constitution of 1933 he effectively became dictator for life. Following a bloodless military coup in 1974, Salazar's successor, Dr Marcelo Caetano, was overthrown and free elections were held.

Two years later, Madeira was granted the status of Autonomous Political Region. A new island parliament would henceforth deal with all issues directly affecting Madeira, except defence, foreign affairs and tax, and for the first time Madeira was allowed to elect five members to the parliament in Lisbon.

In 1986 Portugal joined the European Economic Community (now the European Union, or EU). Generous funding from the EU has been invested in the island's fishing industry and infrastructure. The construction of roads and tunnels, the expansion of Funchal's airport, new hotels, shopping centres, marinas and lido complexes all seem to indicate that Madeira plans to see the tiny island accommodate as many people as possible. For several decades tourism has dominated the island's economy, but Madeira's enduring appeal lies in preserving it as a sublime tropical retreat.

Historical Landmarks

1351 A Genoese map depicts Madeira for the first time.

1418 Portuguese explorers happen on Porto Santo.

1425 Madeira becomes a province of Portugal; sugar cultivation begins, followed by grapes and grain.

1478 Christopher Columbus briefly settles on the island.

1480 onwards Settlers arrive from Europe, including merchants who invest in the sugar plantations and irrigation systems.

1514 The population reaches 5,000. Funchal cathedral completed.

1566 Funchal sacked by French pirates; 300 islanders killed.

1580 Philip II of Spain occupies Portugal; Madeira under Spanish rule.

1640 Portuguese regain their kingdom (and Madeira).

1703 Britain is granted valuable trade concessions with Portugal. Many Britons settle in Madeira and soon dominate the wine trade.

1801–14 Napoleon occupies Portgual; British troops stationed on Madeira; many remain after the Napoleonic Wars.

1850 onwards Writers, artists, politicians and exiled aristocrats from all over Europe 'discover' Madeira. The beginning of tourism.

1872–3 Phylloxera destroys most of Madeira's vines. Bananas replace wine as the island's main cash crop.

1914–18 Portugal fights with the Allies in World War I. Funchal harbour bombarded by a German submarine.

1933–68 Salazar dictator of Portugal. Economic stagnation.

1939–45 Portugal neutral in World War II; Madeira accommodates 2,000 refugees from Gibraltar.

1960 Madeira's first airport, on Porto Santo.

1974 Bloodless revolution overthrows the dictatorship in Portugal.

1976 Madeira becomes an autonomous region with its own parliament.

1986 Portugal joins the EU, gets funds to improve Madeira's infrastructure, bringing roads, electricity and sanitation to remote communities.

1997 Via Rápida motorway opens, transforming island transport.

2001 The island's new airport allows large jets into Madeira.

2006 New theme parks and cable cars open around the island.

WHERE TO GO

GETTING AROUND

Madeira's size can be deceptive. At 57 x 22km (35 x 13 miles), at first glance it might seem that two days would be sufficient to see the whole place. Indeed, fast new roads now make it possible to speed from Funchal to once-remote Porto Moniz in under an hour. But to do so means travelling mainly in tunnels. For a taste of the island's beautiful scenery, there is no alternative but to take to Madeira's mountainous terrain and winding, two-lane roads.

A minimum of three days is necessary to see a good portion of the island; a full week allows you to do it justice and take the time to enjoy its scenic outdoors at a relaxed pace. Until recently, most visitors – counselled not to attempt to drive the island's difficult roads – hopped aboard bus daytrips that took in the main attractions. Even now, although the roads have improved, travelling by car should be reserved for confident drivers comfortable on steep, winding terrain.

More and more visitors are choosing to stay outside Funchal; the offer of mountain lodges and smaller coastal hotels has greatly improved over the years, and there are now visitors who barely set foot in the capital.

FUNCHAL

Funchal is the single town of any size on the island, indeed in the whole of the archipelago, and most of Madeira's historic buildings, museums and sights are located in the capital. With a population of 120,000, it is a larger city than

Views of Ponta de São Lourenço and Baia de Abra from Caniçal most expect to find on such a tiny island, but you can walk across the centre in just 10 to 15 minutes. Exploring inland to the north is difficult on foot, however: the streets become very steep. Nevertheless, walking remains the only practical way to see Funchal: the narrow, cobbled streets were never meant for vehicles, and they can be surprisingly congested with traffic, although some have now been pedestrianised.

One way to get your bearings upon arrival in Funchal is to walk out on the jetty known as the **Ilhéu de Pontinha** and view the city as those aboard cruise ships do. The Pontinha, which was built in 1962, leads round the container port and passes the old fortress (now a café by day and disco by night), which is perched on top of what was once a tiny island known as Looe Rock.

Funchal and its harbour

Funchal's deep natural harbour propelled the city's development in the 15th and 16th centuries, when Madeira became known to expeditions on their way to the Far East and the Americas. The city remains a working port, handling containerised freight, cruise ships, picturesque (and functioning) fishing boats and yachts, and is also home to a small oil terminal, though plans have been announced to relocate the busy commercial port and turn the harbour into a leisure marina.

The Town Centre

The view of the town from the harbour is outstanding: squat white houses with terracotta roofs climb steeply through tropical greenery all around the spacious bay, with rugged mountains forming an attractive backdrop. The dominant building on the seafront is the **Palácio de São Lourenço** (Fortress of St Lawrence). Erected in the 16th century, it guarded the bay against pirates – you can see the ancient cannons poking through the crenellated

Home of Madeira's government
(Governo Regional)

walls. Walking up Avenida Zarco, past the main gate of the fort, you will see the white-gloved sentries who guard what is now the residence of Madeira's military chief of staff.

At the junction of Avenida Zarco and the main drag, Avenida Arriaga, stands a statue of Madeira's discoverer, João Gonçalves Zarco – often referred to as the 'First Captain' – made in 1927 by the Madeiran sculptor Francisco Franco, whose work can be seen all over the city. The imposing **Palácio do Governo Regional**, a handsome building with tiled patios and the administrative headquarters of Madeira, rises behind the Zarco monument to the right. Also on the right is the popular **Golden Gate Grand Café** whose pavement tables are excellent for people-watching, with a view of the cathedral *(see page 29)*. Avenida Arriaga is particularly pretty in late spring, when the jacaranda trees are in full blossom. Along here you will find the **tourist information office** and, next door at No. 28, the **Adegas de São Francisco** (the Old

Blandy Wine Lodge), Madeira's oldest working wine lodge. This atmospheric place was part of a Franciscan monastery built in the 17th century. Here you can take a tour of the lodge (Mon–Fri 10.30am, 2.30pm, 3.30pm and 4.30pm, Sat 11am) to learn about the wine-making process, and visit the wine attics where fragrant wines mature in huge oak barrels. A tour isn't necessary to visit the handsome tasting room, decorated with frescoes painted by the German artist, Max Römer, in 1922 (open Mon–Fri 9.30am–6.30pm, Sat 10am–1pm).

A few steps west of the lodge is the small **Jardim de São Francisco** (St Francis Garden), a delightful urban green space with an open-air café set amid lush tropical vegetation. Across from the park is the **Teatro Municipal**, a miniature Victorian gem that hosts periodic concerts, plays and films. Alongside is the chic **Café Teatro**, one of the main hubs of Funchal's nightlife (late-night disco Fri and Sat most weeks).

Funchal's Sé (cathedral) is one of the island's oldest buildings

Along the street is the incongruous but elegant **Toyota Car Showroom**, once the Chamber of Commerce and worth noting for its fine *azulejo* (blue-and-white tile) vignettes that depict scenes from old Madeira.

Jesuit legacy

The building that houses the University of Madeira, to the north of the Praça do Município, was formerly a Jesuit College which also served as a barracks for British troops during the 19th century.

Towards the centre, at the east end of Avenida Arriaga (at Rua João Tavira) is Funchal's principal landmark, the **Sé** (cathedral; open Mon–Sat 9am–12.30pm, 4–5.30pm; free). Begun in 1493 and completed in 1517, the cathedral is one of the few buildings in Funchal to survive from the early days of colonisation. The exterior has a granite clock tower, but the cathedral's interior is considerably more impressive. It has Gothic arches, a splendid inlaid cedar ceiling of Moorish design, beautifully carved blue-and-gold choir stalls, gilded altars and a sprinkling of nice *azulejos*.

Walking up Rua João Tavira, north of the cathedral, note the black and white mosaics paving the pedestrian shopping street, and explore the pretty narrow shopping streets to the right. At the top of Rua João Tavira is **Praça do Município**, the town's dignified main square, with a fish-scale mosaic of black-and-white stones and historic buildings on all sides. On the northern side is the 17th-century **Igreja do Colégio** (Collegiate Church; open Mon–Sat 9.30am–12.30pm, 4–5.30pm; free), originally founded by the Jesuits in 1574. A spacious and airy old place, it is decorated with 17th- and 18th-century tiles, paintings and gilt-wood carving.

At the head of the square (east) stands the **Câmara Municipal** (Town Hall), which occupies a former 18th-century palace. Don't miss the graceful, 19th-century statue of *Leda and the Swan* in the inner courtyard. The statue used to be

A Flemish St Peter in the
Museu de Arte Sacra

in the old fish market – corroborated by the tiled panel outside the present municipal market *(see page 33)*.

On the square's south side is the **Museu de Arte Sacra** (Museum of Religious Art; Tues–Sat 10am–12.30pm, 2.30–6pm; Sun 10am–1pm; admission fee). It is housed in a 17th-century palace, the former Bishop of Funchal's residence. The outstanding works on view include a dozen or so 15th- and 16th-century Flemish paintings, regarded as among the richest in Portugal and rare even in the rest of Europe. These vibrant masterpieces, as well as other excellent works from the Portuguese school of the same period, were donated to the island's churches by Madeira's wealthy sugar merchants, who during the 16th century traded their 'white gold' in Antwerp, which was then the home of a thriving artistic culture. The main door of the museum leads to Rua do Bispo (Bishop Street) and both this and the parallel street, Rua Queimada Cima, are worth exploring for their shops, cafés and historic buildings.

Continue west from the Praça do Municipio on Rua da Carreira, a bustling street full of popular old-fashioned shops and affordable restaurants. Left of here is the **Museu Photographia Vicentes** (Vicentes Photography Museum; open Tues–Sat 10am–12.30pm, 2–5pm; admission fee) entered via a grand double staircase that sweeps up to the museum on the first floor from a plant-filled patio lined with cafés and shops. The photographs inside reflect 150 years of island life.

Further down the Rua da Carreira is the picturesque Rua da Mouraria, with its antiques shops and the **Museu Municipal do Funchal** (open Tues–Fri 10am–6pm, Sat–Sun noon–6pm; admission fee), another 18th-century aristocratic home converted into a museum. On the ground floor is a modest aquarium showing the sealife of Madeira, while upstairs is an old-fashioned collection of stuffed local sea and land creatures that is popular with young children.

At the top of the street is the charming **Igreja de São Pedro** (open Mon–Sat 8am–noon, 5–7pm; free), built in the 16th century. Its walls are lined entirely with blue-and-white checked-pattern *azulejos* and it has a beautifully painted wood ceiling, fine chandeliers and a massively gilded altar and side chapels.

About half way up the very steep Calçada de Santa Clara you will find the **Casa Museu Frederico de Freitas** (Freitas House Museum; open Tues–Sat 10am–12.30pm, 2–5.30pm, Sun 10am–12.30pm; admission fee). Divided into two parts, the modern wing is dedicated to the history of *azulejos*, while the old mansion alongside is stuffed with paintings of Madeira by 19th-century artists and the furnishings of an affluent 19th-century Madeiran household.

Volcanic stone is used to make mosaic pavements

Continue uphill to the **Convento de Santa Clara**. Built towards the end of the 15th century and expanded two centuries later, it is now a school run by Franciscan nuns, but you can join a guided tour of the convent and its church by ringing the bell by the convent gate (Mon–Sat 10am–noon, 3–5pm, Sun 10am–noon; admission fee). The church is a splendid building, with walls completely covered by rare 17th-century *azulejos* in geometric patterns, and with a fine painted ceiling. The ornate tomb at the back of the church is sometimes mistaken for that of Zarco, the island's discoverer; in fact it is the tomb of his son-in-law – Zarco's humbler grave lies beneath the modern timber floor of the high altar.

During his stint as governor of the island, Zarco lived a short distance up Calçada do Pico, in the **Quinta das Cruzes** (open Tues–Sat 10am–12.30pm, 2–5.30pm, Sun 10am–1pm, admission fee). Constructed in the 15th century, but rebuilt after an earthquake in 1748 and expanded in the 19th century, this is Funchal's finest *quinta* (estate villa) open to the public. The main house is now a museum of antiques, including furniture from a variety of centuries and origins. There are superb 16th-century Indo-Portuguese and 17th-century Madeiran as well as 18th- and 19th-century English pieces. The house is surrounded by a lovely, somewhat unkempt garden of exotic flowers, trees and plants (including a good orchid section). However, the outstanding feature is the 'archaeological garden', an outdoor display of relics from some of the oldest places on the island – tombstones, pieces taken from important buildings and two splendid early 16th-century stone Manueline windows.

Rua das Cruzes, the road separating Quinta das Cruzes from the convent, leads to a lookout point with a view over the town, the port and the dome of the English Church.

The Market, Old Town and Seafront

Between two *ribeiras* (riverbeds) that carry excess water down from the mountains to the sea is Rua Dr Fernão Ornelas, lined with old shops that leads to Funchal's central market. In spring, the little rivers are hidden beneath trellises of blazing bougainvillea. Directly ahead lies the **Mercado dos Lavradores** (Farmers' Market), housed in a two-storey, open-roofed structure built in 1937 (open Mon–Thur 7am–4pm, Fri 7am–8pm, Sat 7am–5pm). The best time to visit is on Friday or Saturday, when fishermen, farmers and traders from all over the island pour into town. This is the only time when the central part is entirely filled with stalls. The market is bustling, fragrant and colourful, with fruit, vegetables and fish of all shapes, colours and sizes. Meat stalls can be found around the outside, as well as several wicker and handicraft shops.

The market marks the start of the **Old Town** quarter (the Zona Velha). The main streets are the narrow, cobbled alleyway of Rua de Santa Maria and, parallel, Rua Dom Carlos I. Once poor and decaying, but filled with character, this former fisherman's quarter has been transformed into a focus of tourist interest, with a seafront promenade, a cable-car

Stalls at the Mercado dos Lavradores

station taking passengers up to the hilltown of Monte *(see page 39)* and an attraction called the **Madeira Story Centre** (daily 9am–6pm; admission fee), packed with exhibits, videos and interactive displays recounting the history of the island. The main focus of gentrification is the row of restaurants that you reach at the pedestrian-only stretch at the eastern end, beyond which lies the **Capela do Corpo Santo** (Chapel of the Body of Christ; officially open daily 10am–2pm, 3–5pm, but actually locked most of the time; free). The chapel, dating from the end of the 15th century, is one of the oldest in Funchal. The low houses beyond once housed fishing families, but are gradually being taken over by artisans making leather sandals or selling lace and embroidery.

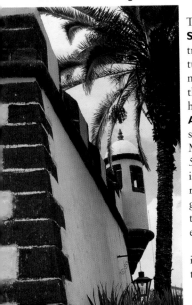

Fortaleza de São Tiago

At the far end of the Old Town is the **Fortaleza de São Tiago** (St James's Fortress). Built in the 17th century and expanded in the middle of the 18th century, the picturesque fort now houses a modest **Museu de Arte Contemporánea** (Museum of Contemporary Art; Mon–Sat 10am–12.30pm, 2–5.30pm; admission fee). There is also a good café and restaurant within the fortress with good eastward views along the steep cliffs that rise to the east of Funchal.

Back on the seafront, heading west, you will not be able to miss the **Madeira Balloon** on the seafront, offering flights that take you high above the city (every 15 mins daily 9.30am–10pm; fee).

Opposite is the **Parlamento Regional**, with a modern debating chamber on the seafront. Behind it is the **Old Customs House** (Alfândega Velha), built in the 16th century. Two blocks west of here, on Praça do Colombo, the **Museu a Cidade do Açúcar** (City of Sugar Museum; Mon–Fri 10am–12.30pm, 2–6pm; fee) tells the story of the island's 15th-century sugar trade.

Niemeyer's work

The architect of the striking Pestana Casino Park hotel was the Brazilian, Oscar Niemeyer. He also designed the adjoining casino, which is built in the shape of a giant crown of thorns.

West of Town

Avenida Arriaga ends at the Praça do Infante, where a statue of Prince Henry the Navigator sits at the easternmost tip of **Parque Santa Catarina** (St Catherine's Park). A delightful hilltop retreat, this park has splendid views over the marina. Aside from the gardens, lake and playground, other points of interest include several bronze statues (including *The Sower* by Francisco Franco, dating from 1923) and, the Chapel of Santa Catarina, said to be the island's oldest chapel (permanently locked). At the west end of the park, the elegant pink **Quinta Vigia** is the residence of Madeira's civil governor. The well-tended gardens are open to the public, as is the chapel.

Above the park looms the startling sight of the Pestana Casino Park hotel. The giant box of a hotel signals the start of the traditional hotel zone, flush with well-known, deluxe 5-star hotels such as the Savoy, the Pestana Carlton and Reid's, plus a few 4-star hotels, *quintas* and posh restaurants.

Just north of Avenida do Infante (along Rua Dr Pita) is the delightful **Quinta do Magnólia** park. You can swim or play tennis in the morning, have a walk around the gardens, and round off the afternoon with tea on the patio. West of Reid's is the *Zona Turista*. Stretching for 3km (2 miles) along the clifftops east of the city, this includes numerous fine hotels and resort complexes and, at the far end, the huge Madeira Forum shopping centre. Not all is brash consumerism, however: a delightfully landscaped seafront promenade extends eastwards from the Lido supermarket for 2km (1 mile), with children's play areas, swimming pools, cafés and well-tended gardens.

Glorious Gardens

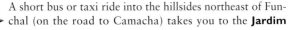

A short bus or taxi ride into the hillsides northeast of Funchal (on the road to Camacha) takes you to the **Jardim**

Clifftop Palace

Standing high over Funchal harbour is Reid's, one of the world's most famous hotels. It was begun by William Reid, a Scot who arrived in Madeira aged 14 in 1836, having run away to sea. He became a prosperous wine merchant in Funchal and by the age of 25 was also renting and managing *quintas* for well-to-do invalids from northern Europe. Some of these villas he converted into hotels, and in due course he acquired the clifftop site for the luxury hotel of his dreams. He died before it could be finished, and the project was completed by his sons Willy and Albert. Reid's finally opened its doors in 1891. In 1937 the hotel passed into the hands of the Blandy family, another famous British-Madeiran dynasty, and in 1996 it was acquired by the Orient-Express group, which has refurbished it without sacrificing any of its *fin-de-siècle* grandeur, and restored its original name, Reid's Palace. It remains the epitome of upper-class luxury, and eminent guests over the years have included Sir Winston Churchill, Charles I of Austria, General Batista of Cuba, and the writer George Bernard Shaw, who signed up for dancing lessons here at the grand old age of 71.

Botânico (open daily 9am–5.45pm; admission fee), the most comprehensive public garden on the island. The gardens have examples of virtually every plant that grows on Madeira and lots of subtropical flowers and plants from far-flung destinations. It occupies steep terraces that offer fine views over Funchal.

The adjacent **Jardim dos Loiros** (Bird Park) has been incorporated into the Botanical Garden and contains all manner of tropical birds. Uphill from the Botanical Garden, the **Teleféricos do Jardim Botânico** (Botanical Garden Cable Car; daily 9.30am–5.15pm, last boarding 5.15pm) offers the chance to glide high above the green ravine west of the Botanical Garden up to the hilltown of Monte *(see page 39)*.

Formal gardens at the Jardim Botânico

Orchid lovers might like to head in the opposite direction, along the short but steep downhill walk to the **Jardim Orquídea** (Pregetter's Orchid Garden; daily 9am–6pm; admission fee). A relatively new project in orchid breeding, it has some 50,000 plants and more than 4,000 varieties of delicate, finely coloured orchids.

Another garden dedicated to orchids, on the eastern side of the city, is the **Quinta da Boa Vista** (Rua Luis Figueiroa de Albuquerque; Mon–Sat 9am–5.30pm; admission fee), set in the grounds of a beautiful 200-year-old villa. This is a busy working orchid farm that has received many awards, most notably from the British Royal Horticultural Society.

But the most splendid of Madeira's horticultural wonders are the **Palheiro Gardens** (open Mon–Fri 9am–4.30pm; admission fee). The hillside estate, only a short bus ride from Funchal to the east of the city, is the property of the family that once owned Reid's Hotel and is one of the famous producers of Madeira wine. Built in the 1820s, the *quinta* has been in the hands of the Blandy family for more than a century. The gardens are famous for their winter-flowering camellias, though the diversity of exotic plants, including a lush array of tropical species, ensures a year-round display. The long, cobbled entrance avenue is shaded by plane trees, while the fields which lie on each side are carpeted with a wonderful spread of arum and belladonna lilies in spring, and agapanthus in summer and autumn.

Lillies at the Palheiro Gardens

Formal and informal areas are landscaped with pools and fountains, while terraces tumble down the hillsides. A deep, wild ravine with thick tropical vegetation is nicknamed the 'Valley of Hell'. Yet the garden retains the distinctive, charming and peaceful atmosphere of the timeless grounds of an English country house.

AROUND FUNCHAL

A number of excellent visits are within easy reach of Funchal. Tour operators often promote Monte, Camacha and Curral das Freiras as a popular half-day excursion.

Monte

The hilltop town of **Monte** has been fashionable ever since wealthy merchants and exiled aristocrats in the 19th century built their splendid *quintas* up here in the cool air above Funchal. Today it is perhaps best known for the toboggan rides

Downhill Racers

Monte's famous wicker toboggans were used at the beginning of the 19th century to carry freight down the frighteningly steep 5-km (3-mile) hill between Monte and Funchal. A British merchant, living in Monte and weary of winding his way down to Funchal every day, hit on the idea that the same toboggans could carry people. A wicker seat was fixed to the basic sled and so the *carros de cesto* (literally 'basket-car') was born. Each *carro* is controlled by two *carreiros*, complete with traditional straw hats, who give an initial push and then ride along until another push, or pull, or sudden brake, is required, depending upon the desired speed and any traffic ahead. For brakes they use the rubber soles of their simple boots.

The modern toboggan ride (Mon–Sat 9am–6pm, Sun 9am–1pm; closed hols) is a pale shadow of its former self (even though the fare of €15 for one person, €25 for two, is one worthy of a high-tech roller-coaster). The road surface is no longer the friction-free, slippery cobbles that had carros careering down the hill. Toboggans now slide more slowly than they used to. And the lot of the *carreiros* has changed, even if their outfits have not. They used to have to walk back up the hill, carrying or pushing the 68-kg (150-lb) sleds, but nowadays they do the journey by truck.

that originate here, though the toboggans now have a rival in the form of the cable cars that link Monte with the Jardim Botânico *(see pages 36–7)* and to Funchal's Old Town (Teleféricos da Madeira; daily 9.30am–6pm, last boarding 5.45pm).

Monte's main square is on the western side of the town, and is a pleasant evocation of yesteryear. The rack-and-pinion railway that once laboured up the ferociously steep hill closed in the 1930s, but the railway station is still here (awaiting conversion to a café), on the western side of the tree-shaded square, and the viaduct arches now rise over the perfectly clipped public gardens of the **Jardim do Monte** (established 1894).

A short walk up a path from the square is the elegant and richly decorated **Igreja de Nossa Senhora do Monte** (Our Lady of Monte), dedicated to Madeira's patron saint. On the Feast of the Assumption, 15 August, thousands make the annual pilgrimage to the church. Others come throughout

Transport by wicker toboggan

the year to pray at the chapel on the left of the church that holds the tomb of the last of the Austro-Hungarian emperors, Charles I of Austria (and IV of Hungary), who died on Madeira in 1922, and whose path to sainthood was prepared when he was beatified by Pope John Paul II in 2004. At the foot of the church steps is the starting point of the **Carrinhos de Monte** – the ride down the hill aboard a wicker toboggan *(see page 39)*.

The **Jardim do Palácio do Monte** (Monte Palace Tropical Gardens; open daily 9.30am–6pm; admission fee), a short walk east of the church, is firmly rooted in the past. The gardens that surround the château-like Monte Palace – once the area's most fashionable hotel – are home to hundreds of plants and various other displays. The entrance fee of €8 is quite high by Madeiran standards, but within the gates is an impressive collection of native and exotic flora (especially good cycads), a koi pond, a porcelain collection and historical artefacts from throughout Portugal, including architectural pieces taken from important buildings and prized *azulejo* panels. The unimpeded views of Funchal are unbeatable.

But in Monte one is spoiled for choice when it comes to fine gardens. There is another situated above the cable-car terminus, forming the grounds of the **Quinta do Monte** hotel. Visitors are welcome to explore the well-tended terrace gardens (daily 9.30am–6pm; free) and take coffee or lunch in the delightful garden pavilion. The last garden is that of the villa in which the Emperor Charles I spent the brief months of his exile on Madeira. The **Quinta Jardins do Imperador** (daily 10am–6pm; admission fee) lies on the western side of the town square, along Caminho do Pico.

Terreiro da Luta, at 876m (2,873ft), has its base about 1.5km (1 mile) north of Monte, but climbs another 330m (1,000ft) to the top and offers another magnificent panorama of Funchal. It was here that the figure of Our Lady of Monte

Curral das Freiras, the 'Refuge of the Nuns'

(now in the church below) was allegedly discovered in the 15th century. On the summit is a monument to Nossa Senhora da Paz (Our Lady of Peace), dedicated to the end of World War I. Around the monument are anchor chains from French ships sunk in Funchal harbour by German torpedoes.

Villages in the Hills

A good half-day excursion by bus, taxi or organised tour is the 16-km (10-mile) trip north on the narrow, twisting road to **Curral das Freiras**, a village that has been isolated from the outside world for the majority of its history. The 'Refuge of the Nuns' is a perfect crater surrounded by extinct volcanoes. The nuns in question fled here from Santa Clara Convent in the 16th century to escape raiding pirates. Protected on all sides – hidden is more accurate – by inaccessible mountains, and supported by rich volcanic soil and abundant sunshine, their settlement became permanent.

The village became famous for its cherries and chestnuts, and the popular liqueurs made from those products: *ginja* and *licor de castanha*; the cakes here are also excellent. The village continued in splendid isolation until the 20th century, when tunnels were bored through the mountains to bring the first roads. Television finally reached the village in 1986.

Curral das Freiras is nice enough but its whitewashed houses with terracotta roofs are best seen from above. The view from the lookout point of **Eira do Serrado** (1,006m/3,300ft) is breathtaking. If you opt for a bus tour, make sure a stop at Eira do Serrado is included (there's also great shopping and an *estalagem*, or inn, here). An alternative view is from the south, across the valley, at the lookout point **Boca dos Namorados** (Lovers' Nest). This is a difficult trek, which, although feasible by car, is usually incorporated on Jeep safari itineraries. From here, the panorama sweeps round and takes in the entire valley (though even at 1,100m/3,608ft you'll still be close enough to hear the bell of the village church).

In the opposite direction, 16km (10 miles) northeast of Funchal, is **Camacha**, a pretty village at nearly 700m (2,300ft). In the heart of willow country, it is the island's centre of the wickerwork industry. Around 2,000 people are employed crafting furniture, tablemats, baskets and other household items. Around Camacha and north of here you are likely to see the stripped willow soaked and left to dry, either by a river bank, propped up against a house, or in wigwam fashion in the fields. You may even see families at

Around 2,000 of Camacha's population work with wicker

the roadside, soaking the willow in vats and stripping off the bark. Most weaving is done at home – the only place you are guaranteed to see craftsmen at work is in the somewhat dingy basement of the Café Relógio. The upstairs restaurant has panoramic views, while the downstairs is a 'wicker superstore'. Camacha is also the starting point for two excellent *levada* walks heading west to Vale do Paraíso and northeast to Eira de Fora. To enjoy these walks without getting lost, you need a walking guidebook, such as the ultra-reliable *Sunflower* guide, available in shops all over the island *(see page 118)*.

WESTERN MADEIRA

Western Madeira begins just beyond the capital's tourist zone. Here, the pace is slower and the coast even less discovered than further east; inland is some glorious countryside.

Câmara de Lobos and Cabo Girão

Just 10km (6 miles) west of Funchal is **Câmara de Lobos** ('lair of the sea-wolves'). The peculiar name refers to the seals that once swam near here. Câmara de Lobos is more picturesque from afar than it is up close. In 1950, Winston Churchill spent time on the island painting the fishing port, an interest that ensured its standing as an idyllic, old-world fishing village. The gaily-painted boats are still here, as is the protected, rocky natural harbour, but the old quarter overlooking the sea has seen better days.

The lighthouse at Ponta do Pargo, the island's western tip

Picturesque Câmara de Lobos is still an active fishing village

The port area has resisted attempts at gentrification and fairly swaggers with macho atmosphere. Hard-drinking locals down *poncha* (sugar-cane brandy, lemon juice and honey) in shadowy bars, while grizzled old fishermen play cards or repair their boats. Close to the waterfront is a small chapel, an early 15th-century project that was later rebuilt (1723). **Henriques & Henriques** also has a wine lodge in the town, where you can learn about Madeira wine (Estrada Santa Clara 10; open daily 9.30am–6pm; admission fee). Otherwise, there's not much for the tourist here, but you have to hand it to Câmara de Lobos for remaining a pure and simple working port.

Beyond Câmara de Lobos, the coastal road climbs for 10km (6 miles), passing through rich agricultural country, famous for the high quality of its grapes. Eventually it leads to the top of the mighty headland known as **Cabo Girão**. One of the highest cliffs in the world, it plummets 590m (1,900ft) to the Atlantic. The views east and west along the coast are sensational. Agapanthus cling to the top of the promontory, and pine and eucalyptus creep right to the edge, but an even greater degree of daring can be seen hundreds of metres below, where farmers have managed to salvage tiny plots of arable land, terracing them on the sides and base of the cliff.

The winding road continues on through the sprawling settlements of Quinta Grande and Campanário. The latter, an important grape-growing area, is also remarkable for its cliffside caves, used by local fisherman for storage purposes.

Ribeira Brava

The next major settlement, heading west, is **Ribeira Brava** (if you are in a hurry, it can be reached in just 15 minutes on the *via rápida* highway from Funchal). The town's name, which means 'wild river' or 'wild ravine', seems hyperbolic for such an orderly and peaceful little community. Except in winter, Ribeira Brava's river is more of a tame trickle. The river heads due north, as does the road – straight across the island to São Vicente – making the ancient town of Ribeira Brava (established in 1440) an important junction.

The main focus of attention in the town is the 16th-century **São Bento** (St Benedict's church), with some of the island's finest gilded and carved woodwork, a nativity and an elaborate font. In Rua de São Francisco, the **Museu Etnográfico da Madeira** (Madeira Ethnographic Museum; open Tues–Sun 10am–12.30pm, 2–6pm; admission fee) is an excellent introduction to the fishing, farming and winemaking traditions that still just about survive in the island's remoter outposts.

The Southwest Coast

From Ribeira Brava, most coach excursions head north to São Vicente *(see page 50)*, as the road cuts through some of the best scenery on the whole island. However, those with more time can continue along the southwest coast.

Bananas are big business along the south coast of Madeira

Ponta do Sol is the next village after Ribeira Brava. As its name suggests, it is blessed with more than its fair share of sunshine. Only during the summer does it really come alive, however, when beach umbrellas are set out on the seafront lido. There are two buildings of note here: an 18th-century church and an arts centre, the **John dos Passos Cultural Centre**, housed in the restored home of the American novelist's grandparents, who emigrated from this village in the mid-19th century.

About 10km (6 miles) west of Ponta do Sol is **Calheta**, a banana plantation centre and the only town of significance as you head west. The Igreja Matriz, the parish church, dates to 1430 but was rebuilt in 1639, and features a handsome Moorish-style ceiling. Calheta is the site of recent tourism investment, with a large artificial sand beach and the **Casa das Mudas Arts Centre**, located on the clifftop to the west of the town – well worth visiting for its bold modernist

Rabaçal, starting point for walks

architecture, as well as for an adventurous programme of contemporary art exhibitions and a cinema showing art-house films.

From Calheta, a steep inland road climbs to the centre of the island, up to the **Paúl da Serra** ('High Moorland'). This plateau measures some 17 x 6km (11 x 3.6 miles), and the flat plain stands in dramatic contrast to the rugged mountains elsewhere on Madeira. The scenery is reminiscent of the bleak moors of Scotland, and on clear days it is possible to see both the north and south coasts of the island. In good weather, hikers are drawn to its remote and barren character. If you are thinking of hiking here, be warned that mists descend suddenly; you may want to go with a guide *(see page 114)*.

Where the road from Calheta joins the main road across the moorland, turn right for the large car park that serves **Rabaçal**, a beautiful valley popular among Madeirans at weekends and holidays. This is the starting point for a couple of spectacular *levada* walks. Both involve walking downhill from the car park along the narrow and twisting tarmac road that leads to the resthouse and barbecue pits at Rabaçal, then following the signs. The flat trip to the **Risco waterfall** takes about 30 minutes there and back. The other takes about three hours and involves a pretty steep climb along the way to **25 Fontes** ('25 Springs') – as the name suggests, a verdant and water-filled spot. Both walks, indicated on almost all maps of Madeira, are wonderfully scenic.

The Northwest Coast

At the island's extreme northwestern tip is **Porto Moniz**, 70km (44 miles), but a world away, from Funchal. A tongue of volcanic lava flowed into the waves of the Atlantic thousands of years ago, cooled and was carved by the sea into a series of protected natural pools. Small plots of land, divided by heath-tree fencing (to protect crops from the salt-laden wind) climb the hills overlooking the sea. With a seafront aquarium and a science centre, as well as restaurants serving fresh fish and seafood, you could spend a happy hour or two here, especially if the weather is warm and you want go paddling in the rock pools or sit on the volcanic rocks and contemplate the ocean.

East from here, the dramatic **coastal road** is one of the island's star attractions. The original road (signposted 'Antiga 101' or 'Old 101') is now a one-way route, which can only be driven east to west (from São Vicente to Porto Moniz).

Natural swimming pools in the volcanic rock at Porto Moniz

Driving the other way you will catch a glimpse of this old corniche road, literally set on a ledge cut into the cliff face. As you depart Porto Moniz, you will pass a rocky outcrop with a hole carved in it like an open window; this has lent its name to the nearest settlement, **Ribeira da Janela** ('Valley of the Window'). After rain, you might also see water gushing down from the mountains and forming waterfalls.

Seixal ('say-shall') is the only other settlement before São Vicente. The Sercial grape, used to produce the driest style of Madeira, grows on steep terraces behind this coastal village, protected from wind and salt-laden air by bracken fences.

São Vicente, perhaps the prettiest village on the island, begins at the point where the northern coastal road meets the north–south road heading 21km (13 miles) to Ribeira Brava. The town lies just south of an unusual little chapel carved out of a rock. São Vicente's compact, well-kept centre is pedestrian-only, and attractive shops and cafés look onto Igreja Matriz, a lovely church with a painted ceiling depicting St Vincent. Tourism is making inroads, and a few restaurants have been designed with day-trippers in mind, but the village remains pristine. Larger restaurants and a hotel line the seafront, but the village itself is set inland, protected from the harsh ocean winds.

Waterfall near Seixal

The newest tourist attraction in these parts is the **Grutas e Centro do Vulcanismo** (Caves and Vulcanology Centre) on the opposite side of the river from the village. Formed when a now extinct volcano erupted more than 400,000 years ago, the caves were carved by molten lava.

São Vicente, one of Madeira's most attractive villages

The 'tubes' formed are more than a kilometre (half-mile) in length. In 1855 an Englishman discovered the caves, which, being a lava bed, do not have icy limestone stalagmites and stalactites but 'lava drops' that look like thick whirls of chocolate mousse. In a low-rise building near the cave entrance is an exhibition centre with some very technical displays on volcanic processes and the island's geology, but also some enjoyable audiovisuals showing how Madeira and its neighbouring islands were formed by the combination of volcanic eruption and the erosive effects of wind and rain (open daily Oct–Mar 9am–7pm, Apr–Sept 9am–9pm; admission fee).

High on a hill above the village is an odd church – actually a clockless clock tower – standing over a small chapel dedicated to Our Lady of Fátima. This isolated spot is a significant pilgrimage place, and can be seen for kilometres around.

From here, the new road tunnels through the mountains back to Ribeira Brava, but the old road continues to cut its way

Changeable weather

Madeira is known for its microclimates. Even though it's a small island, the weather can change several times over the course of the day, or if you move just 5km (3 miles). Clouds come and go with great alacrity, so don't despair if a day starts overcast – the clouds may clear in a matter of minutes.

upwards through verdant countryside until finally coming to a crest at the pass of **Boca da Encumeada** (626m/ 1,007ft). From here you can see right to the north coast and well into the south, while on each side are vast expanses of mountain scenery. This is one of the starting points for treks to Pico Ruivo, which is the highest peak on the island (1,862m/ 6,109ft).

One of the island's best *levada* walks skirts the edge of the mountain and takes in the entire valley, with views of the sea. Look for steps opposite the Café Encumeada. The 45-minute walk along the irrigation canal, more a stroll than a hike, is lined with hydrangeas and ferns and ends at a waterfall. A tunnel roughly halfway along provides cool relief on a hot day.

About 3km (1½ miles) south of the pass, perched on the edge of Serra de Água, is a handsome and comfortable mountain chalet, the best of its kind on Madeira – the **Pousada dos Vinháticos** (*vinhático* is a type of Madeiran mahogany tree) with fabulous mountain views. It's the perfect place for lunch on the terrace, but many visitors, especially those with hiking on their minds, find it an ideal place to stay several days.

The valley on the opposite side of the road, south of the *pousada*, is known as **Serra de Água** and lays claim to the distinction of being the island's first hydroelectric power station. In spite of the introduction of modern technology, however, the valley remains a quiet agricultural community tucked away in some of the island's lushest hills.

The road from here leads down into Ribeira Brava, where the *via rápida* motorway whisks you back to Funchal.

THE CENTRAL HIGHLANDS

The rugged mountain range that splits the island into north and south makes weather forecasting difficult on Madeira. While it is usually warm and clear down in Funchal, the mountains are often shrouded in a wintry mist. But this doesn't necessarily mean that you'll have no view once you start climbing. Mountain tops often jut through the clouds, a spectacular sight in itself. Madeira's microclimates are hard to judge, especially from below. If it looks clear, beat a hasty path up to Pico do Arieiro first thing in the morning. By the time you get to Poiso you should know whether the journey will be worth the effort.

One route to take in a good section of this picturesque terrain is to drive north (and up) from Funchal towards Santana on the north coast. There are beautiful vistas, secluded villages and a range of exhilarating walks en route.

Pico do Arieiro soars above the clouds

Climbers at the summit of Pico do Arieiro

Pico do Arieiro

At 1,818m (5,900ft), **Pico do Arieiro** is Madeira's second-highest mountain but the highest point reachable by car. As the road rises, the rugged countryside becomes spectacularly barren, though plunging volcanic hillsides have been softened and greened by time.

The lookout point at the windswept, Mars-like summit provides a 360-degree panorama. With its stratified canyon walls, a field of frozen lava and rust-red boulders, it's a geologist's dream. During summer, the terrain is parched, while at other times it's often covered with snow. The overnight temperature plunges below freezing most of the year, while the average annual temperature is under 10°C (50°F). There is also six times as much rain here as in Funchal. If the arrival of clouds catches you unaware, take refuge in the café on the summit.

At 1,862m (6,109ft), **Pico Ruivo**, the rooftop of Madeira, is only fractionally higher than Pico do Arieiro, but much less accessible. The peak can be reached by a walk of approximately one hour from Achada do Teixeira in the north, or the classic but strenuous four-hour round-trip hike from Pico do Arieiro. The latter is well signposted and there is a paved footpath, with drops protected by railings. The trek is popular; on a good day you will see several other walkers, so don't worry about losing your way. Warm clothing and hiking boots are essential, though, and in winter bear in mind that conditions on the mountains can be hazardous, with landslides removing parts of the path as well as icy winds and slippery mud. And if you suffer from vertigo it is best not to even attempt the walk.

Ribeiro Frio and the Levada Trails

Back on the main road north (past Poiso) is the enchanting **Ribeiro Frio**, more a bend in the road than a town. Though the name means 'Cold River' this is a sunny and sheltered spot, but if it happens to be cold or wet, pop into Victor's Bar, a restaurant resembling an Alpine chalet, warming visitors with log fires and freshly grilled trout from the hatchery across the road. Adjacent to the restaurant is a tiny chapel and small botanical garden.

The trout hatchery is a series of interconnected concrete pools; the trout become increasingly large as you go along the pools. The botanical garden is not in the same league as the beautiful gardens you will see in Funchal, but it nevertheless claims to have examples of every native species of flower, plant and tree to be found on Madeira, and sprawls unpredictably along twisting paths among shady trees.

Ribeiro Frio is relaxing, but the real reason for its popularity are two **walks** that begin here. The shorter one, 2km (1 mile) to the outstanding lookout point known as the **Balcões** ('balconies'), takes just 45 minutes there and back. After a stroll through the woods, you reach a series of plat-

Levada walk, Balcões

forms that seem suspended in mid-air, with stupendous views across steep hillsides and dramatic ravines to the distinctive peaks of Ruivo and Arieiro. If it's not hidden in cloud cover, the sight certainly ranks as one of the most beautiful on the island. The second walk is one of the island's most popular *levada* trails (*see box opposite*). It continues for just over 10km (6 miles) until it reaches **Portela**, where a good restaurant offers sustenance to weary hikers. The walk takes most people about three hours, so you may wish to arrange for a taxi to collect you at Portela.

An alternative short walk is to head out along the *levada* for a half hour or so (before steep drops begin), by which time you will certainly have been able to sample its charm, and then head back to Ribeiro Frio.

The Road to Santana

North of Ribeiro Frio, towards the coast, is **Faial**, set picturesquely at the foot of the Penha d'Águia (Eagle Rock). There's little of note in the village itself, aside from a handsome church and the Casa de Chá do Faial ('Faial Tea Room') – actually a restaurant, with picture windows and fine rooftop panoramas. The road winds west past several good lookout points for fine views of the village from the main road.

Santana is home to a quaint but primitive style of housing – A-shaped structures known as *palheiros* (very similar to the A-shaped cow huts that dot the hillsides all around Santana). The classic *palheiro* is a two-storey white stucco house with a brightly painted red door, red and blue window-frames and shutters and, above all, a thatched roof *(see picture page 58)*. Two *palheiros*, perfectly painted in red, white and blue, are the objects of many tourist cameras because they are located in the centre of the village (one houses a tourist information centre).

Another *palheiro* that you can explore is in the grounds of the **Parque Temático do Madeira** (Madeira Theme Park; open daily 10am–7pm, closed Mon mid-Jan–May and mid-Sept–mid-Dec; admission fee). Set in 3 hectares (7 acres) of land, this is one of Madeira's best attractions for children, with rock-climbing walls, adventure playgrounds and a boating lake, but also with some good displays on ecology and on the history, customs and landscape of the Madeiran islands.

Levada Trails

Few things man-made on Madeira can rival its natural gifts. *Levadas* – simple irrigation channels that provide direct access to the best of the island's natural beauty – offer the best of both worlds. Cut no more than 50cm (20 inches) wide, and set 30–60cm (1–2ft) into the ground, *levadas* run more than 2,100km (1,300 miles) around Madeira and have been here almost as long as the island has been settled. The footpaths alongside each *levada* were built for maintenance purposes, but they create a great network to explore the interior of the island. Some *levadas* are suitable for all ages; the only requirements are reasonable footwear, a reliable guidebook (such as the *Sunflower* guide, see page 118) and, at most, a taxi waiting at the other end. As *levadas* wind through the hillsides, most gradients are gentle. Nonetheless, paths that follow the lie of the hillside can also give rise to unexpected vertiginous drops.

Santana's unusual *palheiros* are unique to the area

Thatched houses of a larger, more conventional kind are to be found 5km (3 miles) south of Santana, in **Queimadas**, a complex of cottage-style rest houses with attractive gardens. It's a lovely spot for a picnic, although if the weather is clear you might prefer to take the opportunity to ascend to the very top of the island. This is reached by a 10-km (6-mile) drive south of Santana, through the forest park of Pico das Pedras, up to **Achada do Teixeira** at 1,592m (5,223ft). From here, it's a two-hour round-trip walk to Pico Ruivo *(see page 54)*.

The scenery northwest of Santana is just as delightful. **São Jorge** has a richly ornamented historic church, while past the village there is a splendid panorama from the *miradouro* at **Cabanas**, over to the valley of Arco de São Jorge.

The road winds inland towards the picturesque, fertile countryside around **Fajã do Penedo** and on to the pretty village of **Boaventura**. To cool off in a seafront lido, follow the coast road down to the small peninsula of **Ponta Delgada**, where the church next to the lido has a flamboyant ceiling painting of Biblical stories. From here it's just 5km (3 miles) to São Vicente, at which point the road heads south to Ribeira Brava, then east back to Funchal.

EASTERN MADEIRA

The eastern section of Madeira isn't as mountainous as its centre, but it has some wonderful coastal spots, a handful of attractive small towns, productive agricultural fields and a long, surreal promontory that juts out into the Atlantic.

As you head out of Funchal, the village of **Santo da Serra** can be reached via Camacha or from the Poiso crossroads. The altitude of 670m (2,200ft) produces refreshing breezes, and explains why several wealthy British expats have chosen to build *quintas* here and why so many affluent Madeirans still flee the Funchal summer up into these hills.

The most striking feature of Santo da Serra is its flatness; it may not be in the league of Paúl da Serra, but it is still large enough to accommodate a 27-hole golf course *(see page 85)*. Even if you're not much of a golfer, you might still enjoy a stroll through the pleasant gardens of **Quinta da Junta**, once owned by the ubiquitous Blandy family but now open to the public. A lookout point provides views across to Machico on the coast, and you can enjoy a drink at the golf club bar, set in what was once a *pousada*.

At **Portela** (662m/2,172ft), the views of the coast are striking. You may see hang-gliders taking off from a nearby platform. **Penha d'Águia** dominates the northeast coast. This huge rock formation, towering at 590m (1,935ft), levels off to a flat top. The name, meaning Eagle Rock, is derived from the eagles that once nested on ledges in its craggy cliff face.

The village of **Porto da Cruz**, 6km (4 miles) north, lies in the shadow of the rock. Here you will find one of Madeira's

Porto da Cruz

few sugar-cane mills still working, pumping out steam as it processes the sugar-cane to make *aguardente*, the local liquor. It doesn't operate all year round, however, and it is open to the public from March to May.

Machico

Machico is Madeira's first settlement, the spot where João Gonçalves Zarco first came ashore on the island in 1419. Zarco ruled the southwestern half of Madeira, while his fellow Portuguese captain and navigator, Tristão Vaz Teixeira, governed over the northeastern half from Machico. A statue of Teixeira stands outside the town's 15th-century parish church, **Igreja Matriz**. King Manuel I donated the statue of the Virgin (over the altar) and the distinguished church portal. The latter is a fine example of the exuberant style of Manueline architecture.

From Machico's triangular 'square', several streets lead to the beautifully landscaped seafront, home to a small custard-yellow fortress, built in 1706 and now used as the tourist information centre. Its battered walls contrast starkly with the ultra-modern glass and concrete **Fórum Machico** cultural centre nearby. This excitingly contemporary building has an inexpensive first-floor café and a ground-floor restaurant with panoramic views of Machico's wide bay. To the right, as you face the sea, is the tiny 18th-century **Capela de São Roque** (due to open again soon following restoration), while the modern suspension bridge on the left of the bay leads to the **Capela dos Milagres** (Chapel of Miracles) built over the graves of Robert Machim and Anne d'Arfet, the first to set foot on Madeira *(see page 14)*. Beyond the chapel, the town's former boatyard is now a swish marina, with shops and cafés.

The Northeast Coast

The landscape of the extreme eastern peninsula, known as **Ponta de São Lourenço**, is more like Porto Santo *(see page 64)* and the Ilhas Desertas *(see page 9)* than Madeira. Keen walkers enjoy this wild, windswept tip of the island, but for all its wonderful views, it can be a bit too invigorating for comfort.

Close by, at **Prainha**, is the island's only natural sandy beach. Not surprisingly for a volcanic island, the sand here is black; the tiny beach can be crowded in high summer, but is deserted the rest of the year.

Caniçal resident

Nearby **Caniçal** was once a whaling port, but since whaling was banned here in 1981, all that remains of this

Whale Museum, Caniçal

formerly lucrative industry is a museum and a few scrimshaw souvenirs in a hut by the beach. Although the **Museu da Baleia** (Whale Museum; Tues–Sun 10am–noon, 1–6pm; admission fee) shows a video of a whale hunt in 1978, the owner is the epitome of a poacher-turned-gamekeeper. Once commander of the Caniçal whaling station and thus responsible for taking 100–200 of the great creatures each year, he now devotes his energy to saving the whale and other marine life of the area. The 14-m (45-ft) model of the sperm whale is a reminder of the leviathans that once swam in great schools in the waters off Madeira. Whales are still sighted here, but not frequently. Caniçal is still a working fishing port, and has a selection of good fish restaurants.

Journeying back to Funchal from Caniçal via Machico, you will encounter the **Aeroporto de Santa Catarina** (international airport), which serves the whole of Madeira. As you continue driving east, you actually travel underneath the runway, which is supported on huge pillars – a novel, if sobering, sensation.

Beyond the airport is the pleasant town of **Santa Cruz**, with an attractive church dating from the 16th century. Across the main square, the town hall retains a pair of splendid 15th- to 16th-century Manueline windows. A few streets away, the courthouse is another historic survivor, with fine verandas and an impressive main staircase. Along the seafront is the modern municipal market and a pebbly beach, while to the west of the town is the island's only waterpark, the **Aquaparque** (open daily 10am–7pm winter, until 7.30pm summer; admission fee) with a series of slides, flumes and wave pools.

The main road along the coast towards Funchal passes **Caniço**, a village of two halves: uphill is the original village, built around an imposing 18th-century church, with the pink-walled Quinta Splendida hotel just to the south offering the chance to explore its fine 'botanical' garden; while downhill the new Caniço de Baixo is a pretty garden suburb full of holiday villas and hotels set in lush vegetation, with a steep path down to a tiny beach.

Roughly 2km (1 mile) further on, **Ponta do Garajau** is another holiday development, popular with German visitors. The road ends at a fine *miradouro*, where a statue of Christ stands with arms outstretched. There is also a good view west to the Bay of Funchal.

Mural, Santa Cruz market hall

The road dropping down into Funchal winds past some of the town's smartest villas. The first landmark you'll see is the church of São Gonçalo in the parish of the same name; photographers love this spot for its classic views down on to Funchal harbour. Also in the vicinity is the tiny, atmospheric chapel dedicated to Nossa Senhora das Neves (Our Lady of the Snows).

PORTO SANTO

The island of Porto Santo, 40km (25 miles) northeast of Madeira, is the only other inhabited island in the archipelago, with a population of some 5,000. As desert islands go, it's not exactly undiscovered – it is accessible via a two-hour ferry crossing or a very short (15 minutes) flight – but only a handful of foreign visitors find these shores. Porto Santo is still, at heart, the resort of Madeirans, who seek what they have not: sand.

Porto Santo's prize is a long, golden beach, which has only recently been touched by development. But that's not all that distinguishes Porto Santo from Madeira. In summer the smaller island is scorched and yellow, with rusty-coloured rock and cliff formations. The island is mostly quiet, with a short, three-month summer season. Out of season, however, even the main town seems deserted.

Coastal view of Porto Santo

The frequently rough sea crossing drops passengers at Porto de Abrigo, on the eastern tip of the island. (The return crossing, however, is never as bad.) From the dock it is a short taxi or bus ride, or a 20-minute walk, to reach **Vila Baleira** (sometimes referred to as **Porto Santo Town**), the island's only settlement of notable size.

Vila Baleira

The centre of **Vila Baleira** is a small, triangular plaza, comprising a little town hall and a church that has now been restored after more than three centuries of use. **Nossa Senhora da Piedade** (Our Lady of Piety) was originally founded just after the island's discovery during the early to middle 15th century. The present church was rebuilt after pirates destroyed the original in 1667, though part of it, the Morgada chapel, did survive.

Nossa Senhora da Piedade,
Vila Baleira

Porto Santo's claim to fame, beyond its sandy beach, is its link to Christopher Columbus. The town's major attraction is a house, built from rough-hewn stone, that stands next to the church, set back a little off the square: the **Casa Museu Cristóvão Colombo** (House-Museum of Christopher Columbus; open Tues–Fri 10am–12.30pm, 2–5.30pm, July–Sept also Sun 10am–1pm; admission fee) dates from the 15th century and has recently been restored.

The story of Columbus and the Madeiran archipelago is not entirely apocryphal, unlike so many other tales related to the islands. Columbus did marry Felipa Moniz Perestrelo, the granddaughter of the first Governor of Porto Santo, Bartolomeu Perestrelo, but there is no strong evidence that this building was ever his home. That does not stop the museum claiming that Columbus lived here from 1478 to 1480 and that his tragically shortlived son, Diego, was born a *Portosantense* in this house.

Sleepy feral cats, Porto Santo

Regardless of the truth, Casa Musei Cristóvão Colombo is worth a visit. Displays include period pieces, memorabilia, replicas, maps, paintings and sketches, but no personal effects or anything directly linked to the man himself. Another curious enigma about Columbus that has baffled historians is that no reliable likeness of him has ever survived. Take a look at the many different and imaginary portraits in the museum and then compare them with the dashing, modern bust of him in the public gardens by the quay.

The liveliest street in Vila Baleira is Rua João Gonçalves Zarco, situated on the other side of the river from the plaza, running down to the sea. The street is home to the town's small market and a number of characterful old shops and bars.

An Island Tour

Porto Santo is absolutely tiny – less than 11km (6 miles) by 6km (4 miles). It doesn't require much sightseeing, which is good, because most people just come to bake on the beach. Hiring a car is expensive, and what there is to see is usually near the main roads.

Taxis will take you around the island, giving their own tours at fixed prices *(see page 123)*. Pick up a leaflet from the tourist office and ask for a driver who can speak your language. Another alternative is to take a minibus tour with an agency such as Blandy's.

Heading around the island in a counter-clockwise direction, the first stop is the lookout point of **Portela** (163m/

535ft). From here, you can survey the whole 9km (6 miles) of the golden, sandy beach. Head north, however, and the desolate nature of the landscape is inescapable. Crop yields are poor, partly because of the chronic lack of water, and fields that were once tended are now deserted. Earning a living from tourism here is, to most, more appealing than toiling in the fields.

The island's highest peak, at 517m (695ft), is **Pico do Facho**, situated around 1.5km (1 mile) due north of Portela. You'll need to don hiking boots to get to the summit. Its name, 'Peak of the Torch', derives from the warning beacons that were lit here in the days when French and Algerian pirates posed a threat to the island.

The circular road now arcs north to the diminutive village of **Camacha**, where the principal attraction is a picturesque

Camacha's windmill on Porto Santo has not been used since 1993, but is still in working order

old windmill. Nearby, a ramshackle winery with an antique wooden press produces the local Porto Santo wine. If it is closed, you can still sample the wine in either of the village's two restaurant-bars.

A minor road heads west out of Camacha to **Fonte da Areia** ('Sand Spring'), where the rugged coastline is particularly lovely. Sandstone cliffs and rocks have been weathered into interesting shapes and small caves. A spring filtering through the rocks is the source of the island's mineral water, said to guarantee eternal youth.

The main road continues its loop, almost bringing you back to Vila Baleira, before a minor road heads north again towards **Pico do Castelo**. It's only a couple of hundred metres/yards from Pico do Facho, and from its height of 437m (1,433ft), accessible by car, it provides a commanding view itself.

The old, rusted cannons are all that remain of the fortifications that once protected the islanders from pirates. Nowadays it's a popular spot for picnics and barbecues. Porto Santo's airfield (much larger than the one at Madeira before

False Prophets, Magical Sands

The inhabitants of Porto Santo are sometimes referred to by Madeirans as *profetas* (prophets) – the result of a strange episode in the 16th century, when a local shepherd started a religious cult. Not only did he claim to be able to predict the future, he held people in sway by stating he had the power to list their most intimate secrets and sins. Fortunately, the cult was short-lived, and the *Portosantenses* resumed normality.

Magical powers of a different kind are attributed to the island's beach, which is said to hold curative properties that alleviate all kinds of aches and pains. Many Madeirans are convinced of its benefits and bury themselves up to their necks in sand.

Porto Santo's golden-sand beach stretches all the way along the south coast of the island

the latter was expanded), lies just below, and beyond it is the vivid green of Porto Santo's new golf course, contrasting with the tawny hues of the rest of the island.

A favourite local picnic spot is **Morenos**, located towards the southwest tip of the island, though close to, and looking out over, the north coast. It is neat and well-tended with sunshades, flowers and seats, and enjoys a picturesque view over to the tiny **Ilhéu de Ferro** ('Isle of Iron'). The last viewpoint of the tour is **Pico das Flores**, at 184m (603ft).

Directly beneath Pico das Flores is the southern end of the beach and Porto Santo's southwest tip, known as **Ponta da Calheta**. The rest of the island's beach is an uninterrupted expanse, backed by attractive but slightly featureless dunes. Here, however, there are small bays with rocky outcrops and you can enjoy a beautiful view across to the Ilheu de Baixo.

WHAT TO DO

SHOPPING

Madeira is an outstanding shopping destination, given its long, proud craft heritage. The island is renowned for well-crafted wicker items, exquisite handmade lace and embroidery, gorgeous flowers and Madeiran wines. Traditional, labour-intensive methods and quality are still respected in Madeira. Unlike the Canary Islands, Madeira offers no tax concessions for visiting shoppers, so this is not the place to come in search of cheap electrical items, cameras or watches.

Best Buys
Wicker

You'll find an outstanding array of wicker items – everything from linen, shopping and picnic baskets to tables, chairs and trays – throughout Madeira. While many items are attractive and inexpensive, the impracticality of taking them home – especially since wicker is not expensive in most parts of the world – might suggest opting for more convenient souvenir items. Accustomed to exporting, though, most companies will send large items to Europe and North America for you. The Relógio (clocktower) wicker centre in Camacha *(see pages 43–4)* allows you to see wickerwork in the making, an activity more interesting than it sounds: items are crafted with the hands and feet, and occasionally the teeth as well.

Midday breaks

Madeirans do not take a midday siesta, but most businesses, including shops, close for a one- to two-hour lunch break.

Carnaval celebrations in Funchal

Needlework

Madeira's hand embroidery is unsurpassed worldwide. This disappearing art form – still going strong in Madeira – is an amalgam of styles and techniques that has evolved over more than 150 years. Along with fortified wine, embroidery and lacemaking are Madeira's superlative exports, and in Funchal you have ample opportunity to visit factories or workshops where the final touches are put to these painstakingly produced items. However, you're unlikely to see much of their actual manufacture, as the vast majority of the work is done in the home by local women (some estimate that more than 10,000 are involved in the industry). Madeira creates and exports table linens, sheets, dresses, blouses, handkerchiefs and even wedding dresses of extraordinary delicacy. Tapestries range from copies of Old Master paintings to traditional pastoral scenes.

If you're used to machine-made, mass-produced embroidered items, you may be in for price-tag shock: a full set of meticulously detailed table linens can take up to two years to make, so they aren't cheap (although, measured as a reflection of someone's income for that length of time, really they are). If you value the time, effort and craft that goes into these items, the price is likely to seem reasonable.

Handmade embroidery

To be sure that any needlework item is genuine (as opposed to an inferior import or machine-made piece), look for a lead seal (or more often these days a hologram) with an 'M', the emblem of IBTAM – meaning it has been certified by the **Instituto de Bordado, Tapeçaras e Artesanato da Madeira** (Insti-

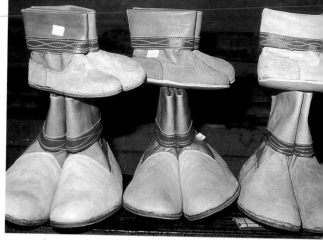

Boots on sale at the Mercado dos Lavradores, Funchal

tute of Madeiran Embroidery, Tapestry and Handicrafts), an official island organisation that has a museum on Rua Visconde de Anadia 44 (open Mon–Fri 10am–12.30pm, 2–5.30pm). There you'll find a tapestry known as the *Allegory of Madeira*, which employed 14 girls over three years and contains an estimated 7 million stitches.

Other Handicrafts

Though wicker and needlework are the biggest sellers, other craft items also make good souvenirs and gifts. **Boots** made from soft goat hide are part of the national costume (women's versions have red leather trim around the ankle). The boot and leather goods seller just outside the entrance of Funchal's Mercado dos Lavradores market is worth a visit. The boots worn by the *carreiros*, the sledmen who push the Monte toboggans, are also available (as are the **straw hats**, old-style boaters, that they wear).

Ceramics and pottery are some of the most popular items throughout Portugal. Most of the items you'll find in Madeira, such as pretty hand-painted plates, planters, jugs and jars, come from the mainland – but if you're not travelling to other parts of Portugal, Madeira is still a good place to pick them up at bargain prices.

Other items include **marquetry,** a recently revived island craft that is featured on small boxes, pictures and furniture. The **brinquinho** is Madeira's answer to the tambourine, in which miniature cymbals are clashed together by costumed dolls 'dancing' round a maypole. You'll find thick **knitwear** – pullovers, hats and gloves etc – at many shops up in the mountains. Unexpectedly chilly weather might make these a good impulse buy. Many of these wintry items are imported from the north of Portugal.

Traditional knitwear

Food and Drink

Madeira cake and wine are extremely long-lasting, so you can safely bring some back home. Genuine Madeira cake, *bolo de mel* (or 'honey cake'), sold in many different sizes, is a far cry from what you get at home. It's a delicious, dark, heavy cake, similar to gingerbread. Despite its name, it is made from molasses, not honey. It lasts for up to a year and goes very well with a dry

Madeira wine. You'll also find plentiful supplies of traditional biscuits, honey, jams and marmalades.

Most visitors take home a bottle or two of Madeira wine *(see page 97)*. Connoisseurs with money to burn hunt down vintage bottles – you can still turn up rare bottles like a 1795 Barbeito Terrantez or 1900 Malavasia Solera (Henriques & Henriques).

Other alcoholic drinks that you might want to take home include *branquinha* (*aguardente* with a stick of sugar-cane in the bottle), or a local liqueur such as *licor de maracujá* (passionfruit) or *ginja* (cherry liqueur).

Collectables

Madeira is not noted for antiques, but stamps, coins, banknotes and vintage postcards are of interest to many collectors. There's a shop specialising in all these items on Avenida Arriaga 75 (Marina Shopping, shop C; tel: 291 223070).

Flowers

Recreating a lush Madeiran garden isn't easy, but you can still take home souvenir flamingo flowers *(anthuriums)*, orchids and bird of paradise flowers (*strelitzias*, or *estrelícias* in Portuguese). The latter in particular will last quite a while after your return home. Most shops will box these for storage in the aircraft hold and deliver them either to your hotel or the airport on the day you leave. Orchid plants and flowers can be bought from Jardim Orquídea, Shop 202, in the Marina Shopping Centre on Avenida Arriaga 75.

Where to Shop

Funchal's central area contains the best variety of shops and local products on the island. The main shopping streets are Fernão Ornelas, Ferreiros, Queimada de Cima and Queimada de Baixo, which together make up the city centre. The majority of Funchal's shops are small and personal.

For the best possible introduction to all of the island's handicrafts and saleable products, visit the **Casa do Turista** (Rua do Conselheiro & José Silvestre Ribeiro 2; tel: 291 224907) on the seafront. The first few rooms are carefully laid out with pieces of antique shelving displaying fragile breakable items; beyond them, you'll find a fairly conventional department store that stocks Portuguese ceramics, porcelain, wines, embroidery, dolls and inexpensive souvenirs. Out the back on the terrace is a 'mini-village', where a little *palheiro (see page 57)*, a house with a weaving loom and an old-fashioned shop, re-create a bit of old Madeira.

Brightly costumed flowersellers in Funchal's market

Competing with Casa do Turista is the new indoor handicraft and tourist market at **Eira do Serrado**. It sells excellent lace and embroidered items, leather goods, and a great selection of vintage Madeiran wine, with bottles dating back to last century (for a hefty price, of course). Next door is the Estalagem Eira do Serrado, a hotel and restaurant with stunning mountain views.

For needlework, visit any of Funchal's factories, which put the finishing touches on items and act principally as showrooms, selling direct to the public. The biggest is **Patrício &**

Gouveia Sucessores (Rua do Visconde de Anadia 34; tel: 291 220801); it offers tours on weekdays. Keep an eye out for other outlets marked by small signs in doorways, including **Bazar Oliveiras** (Rua das Murcas 6; tel: 291 224632) and **Madeira Supérbia** (Rua do Carmo 27; tel: 291 224023).

While virtually every tourist shop displays wicker items, **Café Relógio** (Largo da Achada, Camacha; tel: 291 922114) wins for sheer volume. It is Madeira's 'All Things Wicker', with items ranging from the most conventional to the most implausible.

There are flower-sellers along Avenida Arriaga near the Sé (cathedral) as well as inside the **Mercado dos Lavradores**. A shop specialising in selling and packaging flowers for long-distance transport is **Casa das Flores A Rosa** (Rua Imperatriz Dona Amélia 126; tel: 291 764111). The shop suggests that customers order flowers three days before departure.

For Madeira wines, the most atmospheric place to shop is the **Adegas de São Francisco** *(see pages 27–8)*, in Avenida Arriaga next to the tourism office. It has nice tasting

Colourful Characters

Madeiran street flower-sellers wear traditional costume – not only good for business, but required by law. Ladies in cheerful garb, as colourful as the flowers they hawk, gather alongside the cathedral at the main city market.

Younger girls wear the same red-and-yellow striped skirts, often with a red bolero jacket and red cape, for folk-dance demonstrations. Men wear white linen trousers and white shirts, and red cummerbunds. Black skullcaps, with curly tassels like candlewicks, are worn by both men and women, as are the native *botachãs* (literally, 'plain boots'), made from tanned oxhide and goatskin. Women's boots are distinguished by a red band *(see page 73)*.

rooms (you can even taste vintage wines as old as 1920), a shop selling the three brands now owned by the Madeira Wine Company (Blandy, Cossart Gordon and Leacock), and a book and souvenir shop. Other possibilities in Funchal for wine include **Diogos Loja de Bebidas** (Avenida Arriaga 48; tel: 291 233357) and the **Garrafeira do Mercado Wine Shop** (in the Mercado dos Lavradores). The winery and shop of **Henriques & Henriques Vinhos**, producers of award-winning wines, is located in Câmara de Lobos (Estrada Santa Clara 10; tel: 291 941551).

If you've run out of things to read by the pool, check out **Julber** (Shop 238, Marina Shopping Centre, Avenida Arriaga 75) or the old-fashioned **Livraria Esperança** (Rua dos Ferreiros 119; tel: 291 221116).

ENTERTAINMENT

Madeira does not rank with the Balearic or Canary Islands in terms of lively, night-time entertainment; it's much more of a low-key place than that. Although Funchal has a few pubs, bars, discos and even a well-attended casino with revues, the majority of visitors do not come to the island in search of a hedonistic nightlife.

The nucleus of the tourist nightlife scene consists mainly of the major hotels and their bars and nightclubs. At Funchal's **Casino da Madeira** (Avenida do Infante; tel: 291 231121), in the grounds of the Pestana Casino Park hotel, you can play blackjack and roulette, and take a turn at the slot machines. An admission fee is charged (good for a free drink and chips included in the price); you will need to take your passport if you wish to do more than hit the ground-level slot machines (the real gambling is upstairs). The casino is open 3pm until 3am Sunday to Thursday, and 4pm until 4am on Friday and Saturday.

Nightlife

If gambling isn't your scene, the casino entertainment complex goes for the *tropicalia* quotient with its **Copacabana Bar** (tel: 291 231121), which has dinner shows from Wednesday to Saturday and dancing to live bands and DJs every night. The other principal hotel for nightlife is the Pestano Carlton Madeira *(see page 130)*, which puts on similar themed evenings, plus classical concerts and children's shows. The Savoy *(see page 131)* also has a reputation for lively nightlife in its bar.

Young people head for the **Café do Teatro** (Avenida Arriaga, next to the municipal theatre; tel: 291 249959), **Dó Fá Sol** (Largo das Fontes; tel: 291 241464) and **O Molhe** on top of the fortress in the cruise-ship harbour (Estrada da Pontinha; Fri–Sat midnight–6am; tel: 291 203840). Rua Imperatriz Dona Amélia (behind the Savoy hotel) has a number of restaurants and bars, including **Prince Albert**, an English pub

Fireworks over Funchal's harbour during the Atlantic Festival

Madeiran musician

(tel: 291 235793), and **Gloria Latina** (Rua Imperatriz Dona Amélia 101; tel: 291 225182), which has live music. Nearby, **O Fugitivo** (Rua Imperatriz Dona Amélia 68; tel: 291 222003) is a popular nightclub with nightly Brazilian dancers and transvestite shows (open Mon–Sat 10pm–6am with shows at midnight, 1.30 and 3.30am). **Vespas Discoteca** (Avenida Francisco Sá Carneiro, opposite the container port; tel: 291 234800; Wed, Fri, Sat midnight–6am) has a laser show and lots of sweaty youth.

For more down-to-earth nightlife, two places offer regular *fado* evenings. These are **Arsénio's** restaurant (Rua de Santa Maria 169; tel: 291 224007) and **Marcelino Pão e Vinho** (Travessa das Torres 22; 10pm–2am; tel: 291 220216), a wine bar located to the north of the Zona Velha. *Fado* songs, accompanied by classical guitar, generally deal with the hardships of love and life. Folk-dancing evenings are a regular feature at hotels; and one popular tour is a trip to the **Café**

Relógio in the wicker-weaving town of Camacha *(see page 43)*, where the dancers are reputed to be Madeira's very best.

Funchal's **Teatro Municipal** is the only place that regularly stages theatrical entertainment. It is worth a visit, if only to see the theatre itself. Dating from 1888, it has recently been restored to its original splendour, and produces most of the performing arts. It is the centrepiece of the annual **Atlantic Festival**, held here in June. This festival attracts some of the big names in the classical music world, and the best of the concerts are broadcast on the island's radio station.

Throughout the year, students and teachers from the local conservatoire perform at atmospheric venues such as the Quinta das Cruzes museum *(see page 32)*. Such concerts are advertised in the window of Funchal's tourist information centre on Avenida Arriaga.

Dance Roots

Many of Madeira's music and dance traditions date back to the island's colonisation. They evoke rural and courtship rituals, as well as less happy moments in the island's history. Dances reflect the importance of labour; jaunty jigs mimic the crushing of grapes with bare feet (a practice that has only recently died out) and slower numbers act out the carrying of heavy baskets.

The happy rhythm of these dances contrasts with the overtly somber *Dance of the Ponta do Sol*, which harks back to Ponta do Sol's days as a slave quarters. The steps are short; the feet, as if chained, hardly lifted off the ground; and the head is submissively bowed (slaves were forbidden to look their masters in the eye).

Two musical instruments played are uniquely Madeiran: the *machête*, a guitar-like instrument plucked to a rather monotonous beat, and the extraordinary *brinquinho*, a percussion instrument that features tiny folk-dancing dolls holding bells and castanets.

FESTIVALS

Madeira has four major festivals: Carnival, Flower Festival, Wine Festival and New Year's Eve. As long as you don't mind the crowds, these can be the best time to visit the island.

Carnival

Staged in February (occasionally March), the pre-Lenten **Carnaval** (Carnival) is celebrated in the streets of Funchal with Brazilian-style samba rhythms. However, don't expect the hedonism or sensuality of the type of celebrations in Rio or Tenerife – Funchal is too restrained for that.

Funchal's Flower Festival

Flower Festival

The **Festa da Fiôr** in late April or early May is a crowd-pleaser. It includes floats – decorated in beautiful, inventive floral creations – parading through Funchal's streets. Two events peripheral to the main parade should not be missed. One is the **children's parade**, in which each child carries a single flower and places it in a hole in a 'Wall of Hope' in the Praça do Município. Covered in flowers, the wall is a moving sight. Once the parade is finished, an **exhibition** of the award-winning displays is staged in a lovely old house in Rua dos Castanheiros.

Wine Festival

Festivals take place in wine villages, such as Estreito de Câmara de Lobos, to celebrate the September harvest. You may see grapes being crushed the traditional way: barefoot men and women treading the grapes. Wine samples are also served from traditional goat-skin bags once used to store and carry wine.

New Year's Eve

Madeira's biggest and most spectacular festival has an international reputation. Every year, Funchal's hotels are packed, and you will need to book accommodation many months in advance and pay a hefty premium.Many winter cruise ships anchor in Funchal harbour on December 31 to take part in the party. At midnight, all the houses in town switch on all their lights, opening all the doors and windows, setting the hillside ablaze in light. The cruise ships crank up their flood-lights, and the parties begin. As the New Year rings in, a splendid fireworks display erupts.

Religious Festivals

Several **religious festivals** also take place throughout the year, but one especially stands out. The **Feast of the Assumption**, known more parochially as the Festival of Nossa Senhora do Monte (Our Lady of Monte), is celebrated on 15 August in Monte. Pilgrims flock from all around the island to kiss the image of the patron saint, and some ascend the final 68 steps to the church on their knees.

To the many Madeirans who believe the Lady of Monte has carried them through troubled times, the pilgrimage is an obligation. The Monte church is akin to Lourdes for these Madeirans. The sick and infirm arrive in droves in search of miraculous cures. Once the pious devotions are over, however, wine flows, fireworks explode and *espetada* (kebab) stalls flourish before Monte regains normality for another 364 days.

SPORTS

With no beaches to speak of, and scarcely enough flat ground for a playing surface, Madeira may not be the first destination that springs to mind for a sporting holiday. However, there are sufficient opportunities for most active holidaymakers and excellent ones for those who enjoy walking and hiking.

Spectator Sports

The only sport to watch on Madeira is **football**. Islanders are wild about *futebol*, and two of the island's teams – Marítimo and Nacional, play in the first division of the Portuguese league. Marítimo's stadium is on Rua Dr Pita and Nacional's is high above Funchal at Choupana. See the local newspaper for fixtures or ask your hotel concierge.

The footpaths alongside *levadas* make great walking trails

Walking & Hiking

Mountainous Madeira, with its network of *levada* trails *(see page 57)*, is perfect for walkers of all ages and abilities. Such watercourses exist elsewhere, but nowhere are they so accessible nor do they cover such a great area. The island's irrigation system is composed of some 2,100km (1,300 miles) of channels. The paths that run alongside them are mostly gentle but exhilarating at the same time. More serious trekkers, with cross-country or mountain walking on their minds, can choose from one of the walks listed below:

Boca da Corrida – Encumeada (moderate; 5 hours): views of Curral das Freiras and Ribeiro do Poco valley.

Pico do Arieiro – Pico Ruivo – Achada do Teixeira (moderate–difficult; 4 hours): a trip to Madeira's highest peak.

Ponta de São Lourenço (moderate; 4 hours): great rock formations, flora and views of the Atlantic.

The Caniçal tunnel – Boca do Risca – Larano (easy; 3½ hours): a walk along the north coast between Boca do Risco and Porto da Cruz; terrific flora and sea views.

All of these can be undertaken alone by experienced walkers or under the eye of local guides *(see page 114),* but it is best to know what you are likely to encounter in advance, and a reliable guidebook *(see page 118)* is a good investment.

Advice for hikers
If you're going to do some of the serious trails, take warm clothing, as the weather can change very abruptly. Hiking boots with good support and traction are a good idea to combat uneven or loose surfaces, and sunblock is necessary to fend off the strong Madeiran sun.

Golf

This is a year-round sport on Madeira. The island has 45 holes of championship golf divided between two courses, both of which are esteemed for their scenic beauty. Every spring the Madeira Island Open, part of the PGA European Tour, takes place at Santo da Serra Golf Club. The 27-hole **Clube de Golf Santo da Serra** (tel: 291 550100; <www.santodaserragolf. com>) is one of Europe's most exciting golf courses, suitable for all levels. Designed by Robert Trent Jones, the course is close to the picturesque village of Santo da Serra, east of Funchal, and has stupendous views to the sea below. The newer

Palheiro Golf Club (tel: 291 790120; <www.palheirogolf.com>) is in the São Gonçalo hills, 15 minutes east of the centre of Funchal. The course, designed by Cabel Robinson, has 18 holes and is set in the Quinta do Palheiro Ferreiro gardens. So spectacular are the views over the bay and city that it is a great place to visit, let alone play golf. On Porto Santo, the new **Porto Santo Golfe** (tel: 291 983778; <www.portosanto golfe.com>) is an 18-hole course designed by Seve Ballesteros and located in a green valley on the slopes of the Pico Ana Ferreira mountain, with sea breezes and coastal scenery.

Tennis

Flat land is at such a premium in Funchal that even the likes of Reid's and Hotel Savoy can only afford two tennis courts each. If your hotel does not have its own court, try **Quinta do Magnólia Park** (tel: 291 764598), where the facilities are excellent (including floodlights) and inexpensive. The park also has squash courts and an exercise trail.

Horse Riding

Lessons and cross-country riding are offered by the **Club Ipismo** (Quinta Vale Pires, Caminho dos Pretos, São João Latrão; tel: 291 792582), just outside Funchal. Horses can also be hired from the **Riding Club of Choupana** at Hotel Estrelícia (tel: 291 792582) and the **Quinta do Pântano** (Casais Próximos, Santo da Serra; tel: 291 552577) and on the island of Porto Santo from the **Centro Hípico** (tel: 291 983258).

Swimming

Although much of Madeira's coast drops dizzily into the sea, offering little or no safe access for bathers, there is an artificial beach at Calheta, and there are a number of **lido complexes** around the coast offering swimming pools and cafés, along with concrete jetties that lead out to safe sea-bathing and diving areas. Among the best are the lidos at Seixal, Ponta Delgada and Porto da Cruz. For something more natural, there is the small black-sand beach at Prainha and the bathing complex east of São Jorge, combining a swimming pool with sea bathing and a river pool created in the bend of the São Jorge estuary. You can have a dip in the semi-natural pools at **Porto Moniz** on the island's extreme northwest tip, or enjoy slides and flumes at Santa Cruz's **Aquaparque** *(see page 63)*.

Beach lovers should hop islands to the 9km (6 miles) of sands of **Porto Santo** (though sunshine is only really guaranteed there from June to August). You can either fly on TAP/Air Portugal (15-minute flight) or take the ferry (which leaves daily at 8am; tel: 291 210300).

Most of Madeira's good hotels have swimming pools and there is year-round swimming open to the public at the **Complexo Balnear do Lido** (Lido Swimming Complex; tel: 291

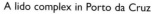

A lido complex in Porto da Cruz

Diving is popular on Madeira

762217) in Funchal's Tourist Zone. There are two main pools, plus a children's pool, sunbathing along the terraces and rocks by the sea, and good catering facilities. What's more, it's cheap. The only drawback is the large crowds in summer. Other good, inexpensive public pools are in the **Quinta do Magnólia** park (Rua Dr Pita) or the **Clube Naval**, along the seafront promenade in Funchal's hotel zone. Some of the larger hotels, such as the Savoy, allow non-residents into their pools, but at a price guaranteed to exclude locals.

Diving

Divers are in luck in Madeira, since one of Europe's first underwater nature reserves was created along the Garajau coastline. Besides abundant, colourful fish, divers can see shipwrecks. Sea temperatures vary between 18° and 24° C (64–75° F). Several diving schools are recommended. **Tubarão Madeira** (tel: 291 794124; <www.scuba-madeira.com>), in the Pestana Palms hotel on Praia Formosa, 3km (2 miles) west of Funchal, offers wreck-, night-, cave- and NITROX-diving. **Madeira Oceanos**, based at the Dom Pedro Baia hotel in Machico (tel: 291 776531; <www.madeiraoceanos.com>), offers everything from beginners' courses and single dives to advanced tuition. Alternatively the **Atalaia Diving Club** in Caniço (Hotel Roca Mar; Caixa Postal 23, Caniço; tel: 291 934330; fax: 291 933011), offers diving equipment for hire and various courses. A single dive costs around €30, while a novice diving course (including equipment hire) will run to €250 or more.

Big Game Fishing and Boat Trips

In the deep Atlantic, just beyond Madeira's shallow waters, you can catch – according to the season – giant blue marlin, bonito, tuna (big-eye, blue-fin and yellow-fin), barracuda, swordfish, wahoo and shark (hammerhead, maco and blue). Madeira's sports-fishing companies operate a 'tag and release' scheme whereby any fish caught are returned unharmed to the wild after photographing.

The very best deep-sea fishing is from June to September. **Turipesca** (tel: 291 231063) charters set out from Funchal Marina. Captain Peter Bristow of **Fish Madeira** also runs big-game fishing expeditions. Contact him at Travessa das Virtudes, São Martinho 23, 9000–163 Funchal, Madeira; tel: 291 752685; <www.fishmadeira.com>; email: <bristow@fish madeira.com>. Big-game fishing expeditions generally cost upwards of €125 per person per day.

Funchal Marina where deep-sea fishing boats can be hired

CHILDREN'S MADEIRA

Madeira has several attractions aimed at families including the **Madeira Story Centre** in Funchal *(see page 34)*, with interactive computers and games based on Madeira's history; the **Madeira Theme Park** in Santana *(see page 57)*, with adventure playgrounds and a boating lake; the **Aquarium and Science Centre** in Porto Moniz *(see page 49)* and the **Caves and Vulcanology Centre** in São Vicente *(see pages 50–1)*. Given all these choices, most kids should find the island an enjoyable experience, especially if your visit coincides with any of the major festivals *(see page 82* and Calendar of Events, *opposite)*. And when all else fails, the pools *(see pages 86–7)* are enough to satisfy almost any child.

If you don't want to hire a car, both the **Jardim Botânico** *(see pages 36–7)*, with its bird park, and the **Palheiro Gardens** *(see page 38)* are accessible by bus. The park on the hill of **Monte** makes an excellent playground, with the added thrill of ascending or descending by cable car *(see page 40)*.

Activities for slightly older children include horse riding and *levada* walks. A very enjoyable nature day – identifying plants and flowers, dipping toes into the refreshing irrigation canals, cooling off in tunnels, picnicking on a hillside – can be had at any of the *levada* paths highlighted in this book. The festivals with greatest appeal for the kids are the famous **Flower Festival**, with its childrens' parade and 'Wall of Hope', and **Carnaval**.

One of the residents in the Jardim Botânico bird garden

Calendar of Events

Madeirans celebrate many festivals throughout the year, some primarily organised for tourists, others deeply rooted in religion and folklore. Many of the celebrations are the feast days of saints.

6 January *Festa dos Reis*: Funchal and elsewhere. Three Kings Festival and close of Christmas festivities.

20 January *São Sebastião* celebrated in Caniçal, Câmara de Lobos.

February/March *Carnaval*: huge festival in Funchal, culminating in a colourful procession on the Saturday before Shrove Tuesday *(see page 82)*.

Last week April/first week May *Festa da Flôr*: Funchal Flower Festival and Ceremony of the Wall of Hope *(see page 82)*.

June *Atlantic Festival*: musical performances at weekends in Funchal's Teatro Municipal and other venues, and firework displays over the harbour.

23–24 June *São João da Ribeira* (Feast of St John) celebrated in Funchal, São João, Câmara de Lobos, Ponta do Sol and elsewhere.

29 June *São Pedro* (St Peter), patron saint of fishermen: bonfires and boat procession at Ribeira Brava, Ponta do Pargo and Câmara de Lobos.

July *Feira Agro-Pecuária*: agricultural fair and festival, Porto Moniz.

2 July Machico celebrates the 'Rediscovery of Madeira' and the first landing of Portuguese sailors in 1420.

Late July *24 Horas a Bailar*: 24-hour folk dance marathon, Santana.

15 August Festival of *Nossa Senhora do Monte* (Our Lady of Monte). Pilgrims flock to Monte from all around the island, some climb the steps to the church on their knees.

Early September Madeira Wine Festival: grape harvesting in Estreito de Câmara de Lobos, with shows and exhibitions here and in Funchal.

8–9 September *Festa do Senhor dos Milagres*: nocturnal procession in Machico honouring the Lord of Miracles.

September (third week) Caniçal: *Festa de Nossa Senhora da Piedade*.

1 November *Festa da Castanha*: Chestnut Festival in Curral das Freiras.

December Christmas illuminations in Funchal, exhibitions at weekends, culminating in a big party and firework display on New Year's Eve.

EATING OUT

Funchal has been catering for visitors since Victorian times. While it's not Portugal's dining capital, there are plenty of good restaurants. For international or haute cuisine, the best places are in the hotel zone, the upmarket, far end of the Old Town, and touristy marina establishments. If you would rather eat with locals, try the side streets around the cathedral, Rua Carreira or cafés along Rua Dom Carlos I.

Most Madeiran restaurants stick to traditional opening times, with lunch (almoço) served from around noon to 3pm and dinner (jantar) from 7 to 10pm. Many restaurants in Funchal offer all-day service, not closing after lunch, and you will never have any problems finding cafés serving snacks all day. For breakfast (pequeno almoço), most Madeirans start their day with a sweet pastry and coffee. Hotels usually serve the standard international buffet, with bacon and egg, cold meats, cheeses, fruit and cereals.

Seasoning savvy

Salt and pepper are not usually placed on the table. But you will be given them if you ask: sal e pimenta, faz favor.

What to Eat

Madeira has its own typical dishes, in addition to Portuguese specialities. As a rule, the food here is simple, it uses fresh ingredients and is served up in hearty portions. A Madeiran trademark is the excellent island bread, bolo do caco, which is made from flour and sweet potato and normally served with garlic butter (manteiga de alho).

Starters. Soup is always on the menu. The best is usually Madeira's own tomate e cebola, a delicious soup made from tomatoes and onions, and very often served com ovo (with a poached egg floating on top). A Portuguese staple, caldo verde (literally 'green broth'), is a thick soup of potato purée with finely shredded cabbage or kale. Another soup from the mainland is *açorda*, thicker still and made with bread and garlic.

Basic fish restaurants serve *caramujos* (winkles), which look unappetising as you winkle them out from their tiny shells, but taste fine, and *lapas grelhadas* (grilled limpets). The latter are a meatier version of mussels (some of them taste almost like liver) and are served grilled in the shell. At the other end of the price spectrum, look out for smoked swordfish *(espadarte fumado)*, a Portuguese delicacy which is a little like smoked salmon, but tastes less sweet and has a coarser texture.

Fish and Seafood. Madeira's speciality, seen on menus across the island, is the *espada*, a fearsome-looking, ink-black, eel-like beast, which can grow to around 1m (3ft) in length and has long, needle-sharp teeth. Despite its appearance, the nasty creature has delicious white meat. Some restaurants

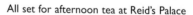

All set for afternoon tea at Reid's Palace

serve it poached, but more often fillets are fried, often with a banana, which complements the flavour surprisingly well. Note that *espada* and *espadarte* (swordfish; *see page 93*), though similar-sounding, are quite different fish.

The other island fish is tuna *(atum)*, a solid, meaty-textured fish served in steaks *(bife de atum)* and often with a Madeira wine sauce *(a Madeirense)*. Maize or cornmeal *(milho)* deep-fried in cubes (also an island speciality) is often served with tuna, and is offered as a standard accompaniment to many meals in *típicos (see page 138)* around the island.

You will find a wide selection of other fish on the menu, usually grilled or fried, including: *pargo* and *besugo*, which are types of sea-bream; *garoupa* and *cherne*, types of grouper; and *bacalhau*, the famous salt-cod, cooked in many ways. It is often served in a casserole, which tends to hide its distinctive, preserved flavour. Try it *cozido* (boiled). Other

Bacalhau, the celebrated salt-cod, drying in the sun

fish are shark, swordfish and *bodião* (parrot-fish).

Two slow-simmering Portuguese favourites that appear on restaurant menus are *caldeirada*, a rich stew made from fish, potato, tomato and onion, and *cataplana*, which is named after the hinged pressure cooker made of copper that is used to cook a mixture of clams, ham, sausage, onion, garlic, parsley, white wine and paprika (ingredients may vary from one restaurant to the next).

Free food?

Most restaurants serve a *couvert* – an assortment of appetisers, including bread and butter, that appear to be free but are usually not. You will be charged anything from 50 cents to €4 for the items. If you do not touch them, however, in theory you should not be charged for them.

Two local favourites are octopus *(polvo)*, served cold in a salad or hot, fried or stewed; and squid *(lulas)*, grilled, fried or stuffed *(recheado)*. Shellfish do not flourish in Madeiran waters, and all prawns and lobsters are imported.

A menu that quotes a price – usually for shellfish or fresh fish – as '*preço V*' means variable, or market, price. Ascertain the day's market price before ordering.

Meat. *Espetada* (not to be confused with *espada* or *espadarte*; *see page 94*) is the typical Madeiran meat dish, a kebab of beef traditionally threaded on a skewer of sweet bay. In many restaurants, however, it is served on a metal skewer with a hook on one end, which is hung vertically from a special stand fixed to the end of your dining table. The beef is first grilled over embers of fragrant sweet bay, having been marinated in garlic and wine to make it tender and tasty – though it can occasionally still be tough. For something easier on the jaw, try pork in wine and garlic *(porco de vinho e alho)*, which is marinated, tenderised and then grilled. Chicken *(frango)* is always on the menu – whether it's served

Locally grown passion fruit

plain, grilled, African-style (as in *piri-piri*, when it's basted in a sauce of hot chilli peppers, then grilled) or in a Goan-inspired curry sauce. Ox tongue *(lingua)* served with a Madeira wine sauce is also a Portuguese speciality.

Desserts. Portugal's *flã* or *pudim*, a type of crème caramel, is common, as is ice cream *(gelado)*. A good restaurant will offer seasonal fruit after your meal, but you may have to ask for it. The island has an excellent range of exotic fruits, so sample them fresh from the market if not in a restaurant. A favourite is *anonas* or custard apple (originally from Peru). Split in half, the flesh is soft and white, with large black pips. To some, it tastes like its name, while others liken it rather more fancifully to strawberries and cream. A speciality of several tourist restaurants is fruit flambé.

Table Wines

There is just one brand of Madeiran table wine, Atlantis Rosé, sold across the island. Most good restaurants stock a full complement of Portuguese wines (top restaurants will also offer foreign labels), many of which are excellent.

Portuguese wines, while not as well known as those from Spain and France, across the board are quite good, and several regions produce truly excellent wines. You need do nothing more than tell the waiter *tinto* (red) or *branco* (white), and you can't go wrong. However, several of the best wine-producing regions have names whose use is controlled by law *(região demarcada)*, and it's worth seeking out wines from the best regions. Dão and Douro in the north of Portugal produce vigorous reds and flavourful whites. Wines from the Alentejo region are also highly regarded.

Vinho Verde (literally 'green wine'), popular in the north of Portugal, is named for its youth, rather than its colour, and has a slight fizz. It goes well with simple fish and seafood dishes.

The two most celebrated Portuguese wines, port and Madeira, are primarily known as dessert wines, but they may also be sipped as aperitifs. The before-dinner varieties are dry or extra dry white port and the dry Madeiras (Sercial, Terrantez and Verdelho). These should be served slightly chilled. After dinner, sip one of the famous ruby or tawny ports (aged tawnys are especially good) or a Madeira dessert wine (Bual and Malvasia, or Malmsey).

Madeira Wine

The history of the island's eponymous drink, famous the world over, is as full and well-rounded as a bottle of the best vintage Malvasia. When the island was first settled during the 15th century, Prince Henry ordered Zarco to plant vines, brought to the island from Crete. Although wine was not planned as an important export trade, it became one of the most important products of the island, thanks to a combination of its notable quality and Madeira's position on the shipping lanes to the East and West Indies. The island was an obvious stopping-point, where water, fresh food and wine could be taken on board. With the rise of the British colonies in North America and the West Indies, Madeira wine was soon established as a favourite on both sides of the Atlantic, and shipped all over the British Empire.

Madeiras of various vintages at the Adegas de São Francisco

Initially, Madeira was not a fortified wine, but gradually the addition of grape brandy became common practice in order to stabilise it on long sea voyages. During the 18th century, it was discovered that shipping the wine actually improved its longevity as well as its flavour. Producers realised that tropical heat was the key ingredient, and towards the end of the century, pipes of Madeira were loaded as ballast on transatlantic journeys in order to 'cook' them as much as possible. When it became impractical to send barrels on return trips, conditions for heating the wine had to be reproduced at home. The easiest way was simply to store barrels in lofts that soaked up abundant sunlight. Subsequently, special tanks called *estufas*, centrally heated by hot-water pipes, were employed; this system is still in use today for cheaper Madeira wines, subjecting the wine to a temperature of 35°C (95°F) for six months.

Oxidisation during the heating process renders the wine virtually indestructible. A bottle of Madeira can be kept uncorked for many months without suffering any deterioration, even when other types of fortified wine (such as port) would moulder quickly under such conditions. For this reason, there are Madeira wines from the early 1800s that are entirely drinkable today.

Choosing a Bottle. There are several types of Madeira, each named after the grape that gives that style of wine its distinctive flavour and characteristics. The lightest and driest is Sercial, which has a full-bodied, nutty flavour, not unlike an *amontillado* sherry. It is best served chilled as an aperitif. Verdelho and Terrantez are both classified as medium-dry and should be served slightly chilled. A tangy aperitif, they are also recommended as an accompaniment to soup. Bual, probably introduced by the Jesuits in the 17th century, is a rich and port-like Madeira with a splendid honeyed taste and an underlying acidity, which means that it can cut through sweet desserts and is also a good accompaniment to cheese. Finally and most famously, Malvasia (also known as Malmsey) is the richest of all, and is usually served following a meal.

Some Madeira wines are made from blends of several years, and the skill and style of the blender is what gives the wines of different shippers their individual character. The youngest component of the blend gives the stated age of the wine on the label: Finest is a blend in which the youngest is at least three years old, while Reserve and Special Reserve wines are at least five and 10 years old, respectively. The best, however, are Vintage wines, bottled after ageing in oak casks for a minimum of 20 years. The longer the wine stays in the cask, the better it will be. The wine is then kept for another two years before sale.

If you really want to impress your friends back home, buy a bottle of 1862 Vintage Bual or Sercial for a mere €450 or so. If your budget doesn't stretch to that, you can pick up more recent vintages for around €35.

Other Island Drinks

After Madeira, the most famous drink produced on the island is *aguardente*, a powerful sugar-cane distillation, which varies in taste from virtually unpalatable firewater to smooth, aged brandy. Look for the term *velha* (old) on the label unless you have an iron constitution. Add lemon juice and honey to *aguardente* and you have *poncha*, a delicious drink that belies its ferocious base.

Other liqueurs are distilled from the island's fruit, two notable examples being a cherry brandy from Curral das Freiras *(see page 42)* called *ginja*, and *licor de maracujá*, passion-fruit liqueur (don't confuse it with the soft drink, *refrigerante de maracujá*). The local Coral lager *(cerveja)* is also an excellent beverage.

If you don't drink alcohol, you may enjoy the bottled mineral water that is produced in Porto Santo, but this can be an acquired taste.

Liquid History

It was Shakespeare who first gave Madeira wine a literary platform, when in *Henry IV* Falstaff is accused of selling his soul for a leg of chicken and a goblet of Madeira (although the real Henry IV died before the discovery of the island, let alone the wine). In 1478, the Duke of Clarence went one better than Falstaff and actually drowned in a barrel of Malmsey. Sir Winston Churchill was once presented with a bottle of 1792 Sercial in Reid's Hotel, then delighted his guests by placing a napkin over his arm and assuming the duties of waiter.

But Madeira wine didn't win favour with just the British. It was used to toast the American Declaration of Independence, and drunk at the Inauguration of George Washington, who was said to consume a pint of Madeira at dinner daily. Benjamin Franklin and Thomas Jefferson were also Madeira connoisseurs.

To Help You Order...

Could we have a table?	**Queríamos uma mesa**		
I'd like a/an/some...	**Queria...**		
bread	**pão**	rice	**arroz**
butter	**manteiga**	salad	**salada**
coffee	**um café**	soup	**sopa**
dessert	**sobremesa**	sugar	**açucar**
fish	**peixe**	tea	**chá**
fruit	**fruta**	wine	**vinho**
ice cream	**gelado**	roasted	**assado**
meat	**carne**	boiled	**cozido**
milk	**leite**	fried	**frito**
potatoes	**batatas**	grilled	**grelhado**

...and Read the Menu

alho	garlic	**amêijoas**	baby clams
ananás	pineapple	**arroz**	rice
atum	tuna	**azeitonas**	olives
bacalhau	cod (salted)	**bife (vaca)**	steak (beef)
bolo	cake	**borrego**	lamb
camarões	shrimps	**caranguejo**	crab
cebola	onion	**chouriço**	spicy sausage
coelho	rabbit	**cogumelos**	mushrooms
feijões	beans	**figos**	figs
frango	chicken	**gambas**	prawns
guisado	stew	**laranja**	orange
legumes	vegetables	**linguado**	sole
lulas	squid	**maçã**	apple
mariscos	shellfish	**melancia**	watermelon
mexilhões	mussels	**molho**	sauce
ovo	egg	**pimenta**	pepper
porco	pork	**presunto**	ham
queijo	cheese	**robalo**	sea bass
uvas	grapes	**vitela**	veal

HANDY TRAVEL TIPS

An A–Z Summary of Practical Information

A

ACCOMMODATION (See also RECOMMENDED HOTELS starting on page 129 and CAMPING on page 106)

Hotel and hotel-apartments *(aparthotels)* in Madeira are graded by the government from 2 stars to 5 stars. Below the rating of hotel is *estalagem*, which loosely translates as 'inn'. These may be simple hotels away from the main tourist areas, or they may be extremely comfortable, personal inns. The categories below *estalagem* are *albergaria*, *residência* and *pensão* – usually small bed-and-breakfast hotels with basic facilities, although a handful of *estalagems* and *albergarias* are the equivalent of 5-star hotels.

Madeira is unique in also offering *quinta* accommodation. *Quintas* are gracious mansions and villas, usually set in splendid gardens, brimming with antiques and restored to provide a standard of accommodation (and prices) equivalent to a 4- or 5-star hotel. They do not offer all the sports or facilities and amenities of a top hotel, but in terms of character and personal service they are often much better. All are limited in number of rooms, so book early. Early booking is also recommended if you want to stay on the island between Christmas and New Year's Eve *(see page 83)*.

Travellers familiar with Portugal might arrive in Madeira looking for a *pousada*, a luxury government-owned hotel set in a building of architectural and historical character. Madeira does not have any official *pousadas*, but the Pousada dos Vinháticos on the north–south road from Ribeira Brava to São Vicente is a privately run hotel that fits the general *pousada* principal, enjoying a tranquil, scenic setting away from the main tourist areas.

I'd like a single/double room with bath/shower.	**Queria um quarto simples/duplo com banho/chuveiro.**
What's the rate per night?	**Qual é o preço por noite?**

AIRPORTS *(aeroporto)*

Madeira's **Santa Catarina** international airport (tel: 291 520700) is located in Santa Cruz, 22km (14 miles) east of Funchal. It used to have one of the shortest passenger runways in Europe until it was enlarged in 2000. Even so, arriving is still an adventure, and occasionally, in really bad weather, flights have to be diverted to Porto Santo.

From the airport to Funchal takes about 35 minutes by taxi or an hour by bus. During rush hour, allow double the time. Several hire-car agencies have service desks at the airport, and elsewhere in the terminal is a small tourist information kiosk, bureau de change, restaurant and bar.

From Santa Catarina airport, visitors can either take the city bus (€2.50), with multiple stops, the airport bus (€4) or a taxi, which has posted set fares (between €20 and €30 depending on the time of day) to Funchal's tourist or hotel zone, or city centre.

There are frequent daily flights from Madeira to the airport at **Porto Santo** (tel: 291 980120). All these flights are operated by TAP Air Portugal (<www.flytap.com>). There are also some direct flights to Porto Santo from Lisbon and Oporto.

Where can I get a taxi?	**Onde posso encontrar um táxi?**
How much is it to central Funchal?	**Quanto custa para ir ao centro de Funchal?**
Does this bus go to Funchal?	**Vai para Funchal este autocarro?**

B

BICYCLE HIRE *(aluguel de bicicleta)*

You can rent a mountain bike, motor scooter or motorcycle from **Joyride** (tel: 291 234906; <www.madeiramotorbikes.com>) at Shop 210–11 in the Olimpo shopping mall on Avenida do Infante in Funchal. Mountain bikes cost from €11 a day, scooters from €24 a day.

BUDGETING FOR YOUR TRIP

With a favourable exchange rate, Madeira may well be cheaper than many other European island destinations.

Getting to Madeira. There are regular scheduled and charter flights that go direct to Madeira from many European cities. Return (round-trip) flights from London are likely to cost anywhere from £200 to £400. If you are travelling from beyond Europe, the flight will be a considerably greater portion of your overall budget – probably at least $1000 from North America. Economical package deals – flights and hotel – are usually available. Until direct flights begin, flights from North America (and many European cities) go through Lisbon.

Accommodation. Hotels at the top levels are comparable to those in large European cities. Many of the 2-, 3- and 4-star rating are comparatively good value. A double room with bath per night in a 3-star averages €45–75; 4-star, €60–120; 5-star, €125–200.

Meals. Even top-rated restaurants may be surprisingly affordable compared to most European capitals. Portuguese wines are quite good and very attractively priced, even in fine restaurants. A three-course meal with wine in a reasonable establishment averages €12.50–25 per person. Many hotels offer half- and full-board plans.

Local transport. Buses and taxis are reasonable. A bus to the centre of Funchal from the hotel or tourist zone is about €1.60; a 7-day pass costs €15; a taxi costs about €5 (add a fare supplement of 20 percent at weekends, public holidays and between 10pm and 7am).

Incidentals. Your major expenses will be excursions, entertainment and daytime sporting activities. Hiring a car is a good idea to allow maximum flexibility: economy car hire will cost between €25 and €40 per day (including collision insurance and taxes); petrol is around €1.50 per litre, diesel around €1.60.

Nightclub and disco cover charges are high, and some clubs have a minimum consumption policy of around €150. Casino (admission only) is €4; casino entrance plus a show and dinner costs €40. Gamblers would be wise to budget for the possibility of losses. A folklore or *fado* show, including dinner, runs at €25–40 per person.

Madeira coach trips from Funchal cost about €30 for a half day, €50 for a full day. Island-hopping to Porto Santo by air is about €75 return; by ferry, €50 return.

C

CAMPING *(campismo)*

There are two regular camp sites on the Madeira archipelago, one in Porto Moniz and the other on Porto Santo, in Vila Baleira. A third, in the Montado do Pereiro nature reserve on the slopes above Funchal, requires prior permission and authorisation from the Madeira Camping service. For more details contact: **Parque de Campismo do Porto Santo** (Vila Baleira, 9400 Porto Santo, Madeira; tel: 291 982160) or the **Madeira Camping Service** (Estrada Monumental/ Hotel Baía Azul; tel: 291 776726; fax: 291 762003; email: <info@ madeira-camping.com>) or visit <www.madeira-camping.com>.

| Is there a campsite near here? | **Há algum parque de campismo por aqui perto?** |
| May we camp here? | **Podemos acampar aqui?** |

CAR HIRE *(carros de aluguer)* (See also DRIVING on page 110 and BUDGETING FOR YOUR TRIP on page 105)

There are both local and major international car hire agencies in Funchal (most near the hotel and tourist zones) and at the airport. Prices vary significantly, so shop around – local firms tend to be cheaper and less prone to charging extra for scratches or dents.

You must be at least 21 and have held a valid national (or international) driving licence for at least one year. You will need to present a recognised credit card when booking. Third-party fire and theft insurance is included in the basic charge, but most firms quote collision damage waiver (CDW) as an extra (usually €6–7.50 per day). Without this, you could be liable for any damage or loss to your vehicle, however caused, so you are strongly advised to accept it. Check with your credit-card company before departure to verify what it covers when used to pay for the rental (many will cover the collision damage waiver and theft of vehicle protection). A government tax of 12 percent is added to the total bill when booking locally.

An economy hire (such as a Nissan Micra) starts at €175 per week. Major internationl agents are: **Avis** (Largo António Nobre 164; tel: 291 764546); **Europcar** (Estrada Monumental 306; tel: 291 765116); **Hertz** (Estrada Monumental 284; tel: 291 764410); and **Sixt** (Estrada Monumental 182; tel: 764221).

I'd like to hire a car	**Queria alugar um carro**
…tomorrow	**…para amanhã**
…for one day/one week	**…por um dia/uma semana**
Please include full insurance.	**Que inclua um seguro contra todos os riscos, por favor.**

CLIMATE (clima)

Madeira is generally warm and spring-like all year, making it an excellent winter retreat for northern Europeans. However, the winter months can be relatively wet and the winds noticeably stronger. The rainiest period is from October to December, with an average of 6 to 7 days of rain per month, but you can still usually count on an average of 6 hours of sunshine a day. From May to September, the air is warm and somewhat humid. The typical pattern, year-round, is a clear, bright morning, with clouds rolling down from the mountains in the afternoon.

For warm, clear weather, ideal for mountain walking, summer is your best bet.

Average daily temperature

	J	F	M	A	M	J	J	A	S	O	N	D
°C	17	17	17	17	18	19	20	21	22	23	20	18
°F	63	63	63	63	64	66	68	70	72	73	68	64

Sea temperature

	J	F	M	A	M	J	J	A	S	O	N	D
min °C	13	13	13	14	16	17	19	19	19	18	16	14
max °C	19	18	19	19	21	22	24	24	24	23	22	19
min °F	56	56	56	58	60	63	66	67	67	65	61	58
max °F	66	65	66	67	69	72	75	76	76	74	71	67

CLOTHING (roupa)

Warm-weather clothes will be fine in summer, but even then pack a pullover for mountain excursions. Winters are mild with the occasional shower, so a light, rainproof jacket may come in handy. In winter, you will definitely need warm, waterproof clothes for inland trips. If you're planning on walking you will need sensible footwear, but unless you are intent on tackling some of the more arduous trails, you won't need hiking boots.

Madeira has long been a place where visitors dress up for tea and formal dinners. Although there's less formality these days – shorts and T-shirts are fine during the day – Reid's formal restaurants still require men to wear a dark suit and tie. At other luxury hotels and restaurants, jacket and tie are generally expected. Nightspots such as the casino are more relaxed, and a jacket and tie are no longer the rule.

Will I need a tie?	**É preciso gravata?**
Is it all right if I wear this?	**Vou bem assim?**

CRIME AND SAFETY *(delito)*

(See also EMERGENCIES on page 113 and POLICE on page 121)

Although Madeira is one of the safest places in the world for tourists, factors such as poverty (which does exist here, especially in small villages) inevitably make temptation irresistible for some, and there have been some recent problems with drug addicts mugging walkers along lonely *levada* trails. Follow the same general rules that you would elsewhere. Never leave anything of value in your car, even if it is out of sight. Burglaries of holiday apartments are rare, but leave any valuables in a safe-deposit box, or with the hotel reception. You must report any losses to the local police within 24 hours and obtain a copy of your statement for insurance purposes.

I want to report a theft.   **Quero participar um roubo.**

CUSTOMS AND ENTRY REQUIREMENTS *(alfândega/visto)*

UK citizens, Americans, Canadians and many other nationalities need only a passport valid for 6 months – no visa – to visit Portugal. EU nationals (except from the UK) may enter with an identity card. The length of stay authorised for most tourists is 90 days (60 for US and Canadian citizens).

Currency restrictions. Visitors from abroad can bring into Portugal (or depart with) any amount of euros or foreign currency.

Customs. Madeira is part of the EU, but has separate duty-free status within Portugal. You can import duty-free: 200 cigarettes or 50 cigars or 250g of tobacco; 1 litre of spirits; 2 litres of wine; 50g of perfume and 250ml of eau de toilette.

I've nothing to declare.   **Não tenho nada a declarar.**
It's for my personal use.   **É para uso pessoal.**

D

DRIVING

There are many good reasons not to drive on Madeira: car hire and petrol are not cheap, but taxis are, and the tortuous mountain roads can be hard on one's nerves. But you may well enjoy the challenge of the winding roads and, of course, you have maximum flexibility with your own set of wheels.

Road conditions. It is only worth considering driving into Funchal if you are staying well outside the town (at Machico or Garajau, for instance). If you do, expect traffic jams. The roads across the island offer a choice between fast modern highways, often enclosed in tunnels, or scenic but slow mountain roads that can be murderously twisting. The latter demand confident, relaxed drivers.

Rules and regulations. The rules are the same as on the Continent: drive on the right, overtake on the left, give right of way to all vehicles coming from your right. Speed limits are nominally 110kph (68mph) on highways, 90kph (56mph) outside built-up areas and 50kph (30mph) in built-up areas. Average cross-country speeds are well below 60kph (37mph). Seatbelts must be worn, and children under 12 are not allowed in the front seats. Motorcycle helmets should also be worn at all times.

Fuel costs. Unleaded petrol is around €1.50 per litre, diesel is around €1.60. Prices, controlled by the government, should be the same – or very close to it – everywhere you go. Many petrol stations are 24-hour, and all accept credit cards.

Parking. Funchal is served by reasonably priced car parks at either end of town. Parking in the centre is virtually impossible, except the 'blue zone' (metered parking) along Avenida do Mar e das Comunidades Madeirenses (facing the Marina). You will have few difficulties elsewhere on the island.

Road signs. Apart from the standard international pictographs, you may encounter the following:

Alto	Stop
Cruzamento	Crossroads
Curva perigosa	Dangerous bend/curve
Descida íngreme	Steep hill
Desvio	Detour
Encruzilhada	Crossing
Estacionamento permitido	Parking permitted
Estacionamento proibido	No parking
Guiar com cuidado	Drive with care
Máquinas em manobras	Men working
Obras/Trabalhos	Men working
Paragem (de autocarro)	Bus stop
Pare	Stop
Pedestres, peões	Pedestrians
Perigo	Danger
Proibida a entrada	No entry
Seguir pela direita/esquerda	Keep right/left
Sem saída	No through road
Are we on the right road for...?	**É esta estrada para...?**
Fill it up, please, with...	**Encha, por favor, de...**
three star/four star/	**normal/super/**
unleaded/diesel	**sem chumbo/gasóleo**
My car's broken down	**O meu carro está avariado**
There's been an accident	**Houve um acidente**

If you need help. If you are driving a hired car, the car-hire company will give you a number to contact in case of breakdown or emergency. If you belong to a motoring organisation affiliated to the **Automóvel Clube de Portugal** (ACP), you can make use of its services free of charge. The Funchal office is at Rua Dr António José Almeida 17-2°; tel: 291 223659. You will have no problem finding well-equipped garages in Madeira.

E

ELECTRICITY *(corrente eléctrica)*

The standard current is 220-volt, 50Hz AC. For US appliances, 220v transformers and plug adaptors are needed.

I need an adaptor/ a battery, please.	**Preciso de um adaptador/ uma pilha, por favor.**

EMBASSIES AND CONSULATES *(embaixada; consulado)*

Several countries maintain consulates in Funchal:

UK Consulate (also for Commonwealth citizens): Avenida de Zarco 2; tel: 291 212860; email:<brit.confunchal@mail.eunet.pt>.

US Consular Agency: Rua da Alfandega 10; tel: 291 235636.

For serious matters, contact your embassy in Lisbon:

Australia (Embassy) Avenida da Liberdade 200; tel: 21 310 1500.

Canada (Embassy/Consulate) Avenida da Liberdade 198–200, 3°; tel: 21 316 4600.

Republic of Ireland (Embassy/Consulate) Rua da Imprensa à Estrela 1–4; tel: 21 392 9440.

South Africa (Embassy) Avenida Luis Bívar 10; tel: 21 319 2200.

UK (Embassy) Rua de São Bernardo 33; tel: 21 392 4400.

US (Embassy/Consulate) Avenida das Forças Armadas 16; tel: 21 727 2122.

Most embassies and consulates are open Mon–Fri, from 8am to noon and 2 to 4pm.

Where is the British/ American embassy?	**Onde é a embaixada inglesa/ americana?**

EMERGENCIES *(urgência)*
(See also HEALTH AND MEDICAL CARE on page 115)

The emergency number for police, fire or ambulance is **112**. Funchal hospital has a 24-hour emergency ward; tel: 291 705666. Outside Funchal, ask for the local *Centro de Saúde* (Health Centre).

G

GAY AND LESBIAN TRAVELLERS

A website, <www.portugalgay.pt>, contains a travel guide for gays and lesbians, with information in English and other languages. It has little specific information relating to Madeira, but has a message board for postings.

GETTING THERE (See also AIRPORT on page 104)

Air Travel. There are frequent charter flights to Madeira from international and regional airports in the UK and from international airports in Austria, France, Germany, Spain and Scandinavia. British Airways (<www.ba.com>) flies directly to Madeira from London Gatwick. The national Portuguese airline is TAP/Air Portugal (<www. flytap.com>), which flies from several European cities to Funchal via Lisbon or Porto. For cheaper airfares, check with Easyjet (<www.easyjet.com>), which provides budget, 'no-frills' flights to Funchal from two airports in the UK, Bristol and London Stansted.The flight time from London to Madeira is approximately 3 hours 30 minutes, and from Lisbon to Madeira about 1 hour 30 minutes.

As well as these scheduled airline operators, many charter flights connect Madeira to mainland Europe and are considerably less expensive than scheduled flights.

It is no longer possible to sail to Madeira by cargo ship. Big cruise liners stop off at the island, but often only long enough for a brief sightseeing tour.

GUIDES AND TOURS (See PUBLIC TRANSPORT on page 122)

One of the preferred ways of seeing Madeira is by coach or minibus tour. Several operators go to the same places, but charge different rates for different services. Itineraries include: West of the Island; East of the Island, including Pico do Arieiro; a half-day covering Monte/Curral das Freiras/ Picos dos Barcelos; guided *levada* walks; and Jeep Safaris to out-of-the-way places such as Boca dos Namorados *(see page 43)* or Paúl da Serra *(page 48)*. Not all of these are good value; the Monte trip is simple and inexpensive to do by yourself, as are the *levada* walks. Other itineraries offer a day-trip to Porto Santo, including an island tour (this is only recommended in summer, when sunshine and calm sailing are the norm), but you can also make your own way to the island and take a half-day minibus tour. Half-day boat trips cruise up and down the Madeiran coast, and other outings from Funchal Marina include a trip to the Ilhas Desertas, or a full day's sailing, including lunch and wine.

Information on tour operators, including Blandy's and other agencies, is available from the Funchal tourism information office *(see page 127)* and most hotels. Highly recommended are **Lido Tours** (also known as Strawberry World; Centro Commercial Monumental Lido; tel: 291 762429; fax: 291 762433; email: <tours@strawberry-world. com>; <www.strawberry-world.com>), which offers small-size island tours in minibuses, *levada* walks and mountain walks.

Madeira Explorers focuses on guided outdoor ecotourism (Centro Commercial Monumental Lido, Shop 5, 3rd Floor; tel: 291 763701; fax: 291 761464; email: <info@madeira-explorers.com; <www.madeira-levada-walks.com>). **Nature Meetings** specialises in guided walks on Madeira, which you can do as part of a group, or individually, with transport provided at the start and end of the walk

We'd like an English-speaking   **Queremos um guia que fale**
guide/an English interpreter.   **inglês/um intérprete de inglês.**

(tel: 291 524482; fax: 291 524484; email:<info@naturemeetings.com>; <www.naturemeetings.com>. **Terras de Aventura** specialises in adventure sports on Madeira, including walking, canoeing, watersports, hang-gliding and mountain biking (Caminho do Amparo 25, Funchal; tel: 291 708990; fax: 291 708999; email: <reservationas@ terrasdeaventura.com>; <www.terrasdeaventura.com>).

H

HEALTH AND MEDICAL CARE *(saúde)*
(See also EMERGENCIES on page 113)

There are 67 health centres situated around the Madeira island, and one at Porto Santo. *Farmácias* (chemists/drugstores) are open Mon–Fri 9am–1pm and 3–7pm, Sat 9am–1pm. On the door of every pharmacy you will find postings of after-hours chemists.

Tourist offices carry lists of doctors and dentists who speak English. For more serious illness or injury, **Hospital Cruz de Carvalho** (Avenida Luis de Camoes 57; tel: 291 705666) is the island's largest hospital and has English-speaking staff. In an emergency, dial **112** for an ambulance.

Medical insurance to cover illness or accident while abroad is a good idea. EU nationals with a European Health Insurance Card (EHIC) obtained before departure can receive free emergency treatment at Social Security and Municipal hospitals in Madeira; private

Where's the nearest (all night) pharmacy?	Onde fica a farmácia (de serviço) mais próxima?
I need a doctor/dentist	Preciso de um médico/dentista
an ambulance	uma ambulância
hospital	hospital
An upset stomach	Dôr de estômago
Sunburn/a fever	Queimadura de sol/febre

hospitals are expensive. If you don't take the EHIC with you, you must pay on the spot and make a claim on your travel insurance later.

The most likely illness to befall travellers will be due to an excess of sun or alcohol. Madeiran tap water *(água)* is safe and tastes pretty good. Bottled mineral water is sold everywhere.

Mosquitoes are present in summer, so an anti-mosquito device that plugs into your wall and emits a vapour that is noxious to the insect, but not to you, is worthwhile (available at airport shops).

HOLIDAYS *(feriado)*

The following is a list of national holidays in Portugal.

1 January	**Ano Novo**	New Year's Day
25 April	**Dia da Liberdade**	Freedom Day
1 May	**Dia do Trabalho**	Labour Day
10 June	**Dia de Portugal**	National Day
15 August	**Assunção**	Assumption
5 October	**Dia da República**	Republic Day
1 November	**Todos os Santos**	All Saints' Day
1 December	**Restuaração/Dia da Independência**	Day of Restoration/ Independence
8 December	**Imaculada Conceição**	Immaculate Conception
25 December	**Natal**	Christmas Day

Movable dates:

Carnaval	Shrove Tuesday/Carnival
Sexta-feira Santa	Good Friday
Corpo de Cristo	Corpus Christi

Madeira also celebrates 1 July (Madeira Autonomous Region Day), 21 August (municipal holiday) and 26 December (Boxing Day).

Are you open (closed) tomorrow?	**Estão abertos (encerrados) amanhã?**

L

LANGUAGE

The official language is Portuguese. Basic Spanish should help with reading signs and menus, but is unlikely to unlock the mysteries of spoken Portuguese. The Portuguese spoken in Madeira and the rest of Portugal is more gutteral-sounding, as well as faster, than that spoken in Brazil.

Here are some useful phrases to get you going (see also the front cover flap of this guide):

Good day/afternoon/evening	**Bom dia/Boa tarde/Boa noite**
Goodbye	**Adeus**
please	**faz favor (por favor)**
thank you	**obrigado/obrigada (male/female speaker)**
How do you do/Pleased to meet you	**Muito prazer**
How are you?	**Como está?**
Very well, thank you	**Muito bem, obrigado/obrigada**
What does this mean?	**Que quer dizer isto?**
Please write it down	**Escreva-mo, por favor**
where/when/how?	**onde/quando/como?**
how long/how far?	**quanto tempo/a que distância?**
left/right	**esquerdo/direito**
cheap/expensive	**barato/caro**
hot/cold	**quente/frio**
old/new	**velho/novo**
open/closed	**aberto/fechado**
vacant/occupied	**livre/ocupado**
early/late	**cedo/tarde**
Help me, please	**Ajude-me, por favor**

day/week/month/year	**dia/semana/mês/ano**
yesterday/today/tomorrow	**ontem/hoje/amanhã**
Sunday	**domingo**
Monday	**segunda-feira**
Tuesday	**terça-feira**
Wednesday	**quarta-feira**
Thursday	**quinta-feira**
Friday	**sexta-feira**
Saturday	**sábado**
What day is it today?	**Que dia é hoje?**

The *Berlitz Portuguese Phrasebook and Dictionary* covers most situations you're likely to encounter during a visit to Portugal. Also useful is the *Berlitz Portuguese–English/English–Portuguese Pocket Dictionary*, containing a special menu-reader supplement.

M

MAPS

Madeira is a small island with relatively few roads, so orientation is easy. The tourist information offices in Funchal and Porto Santo will supply you with a free map that includes both the island and capital and shows several of the most popular *levada* trails. For almost all purposes, even driving across the whole of the island, the free map should be sufficient. However, more detailed maps are published by the Instituto Geográfico e Cadastral, obtainable at local bookshops. Few maps are up to date because of the rapid pace of road building. The best map available in the UK is the Madeira Tour and Trail Map, <www.walking.demon.co.uk>. Those intent on doing some serious walking should buy a copy of *Landscapes of Madeira* by John and Pat Underwood (Sunflower Books; <www.sunflowerbooks.co.uk>), which includes specially drawn walking tour maps and details many *levada* trails.

MEDIA *(jornal; revista; radio; televisão)*

Europe's principal papers, including most British dailies, are on the newsstands the day after publication. *The International Herald Tribune* and in some places *USA Today* appear on the day of publication. Popular foreign magazines are sold at many kiosks. The only local English-language publication is the free monthly, *The Madeira Island Bulletin* (also available in German as *Madeira Aktuell*). You can pick up a copy at the tourist office in Funchal. If you can understand a little Portuguese, the daily *Notícias da Madeira* newspaper gives you a weather forecast and museum and temporary exhibition details, among other things.

Madeira has its own TV channel and also receives programmes from mainland Portugal. Most large hotels and some bars also have satellite TV for screening football matches and other sporting events. For details of what's on, pick up a copy of the *Notícias da Madeira*.

Tune into Tourist Radio (96 FM) for news and features of tourist interest on the island, broadcast in several languages (English, 5.45–6.30pm Mon–Fri). The BBC World Service and Voice of America can be heard on shortwave.

Have you any English-language newspapers/magazines?	**Tem jornais/ revistas em inglês?**

MONEY MATTERS *(dinheiro)*
(See also BUDGETING FOR YOUR TRIP on page 105)

Currency *(moeda)*. In common with most other European countries, the euro (EUR) is the official currency used in Portugal. Notes are denominated in 5, 10, 20, 50, 100 and 500 euros; coins in 1 and 2 euros and 1, 2, 5, 10, 20 and 50 cents.

Currency exchange *(banco; câmbio)*. Normal banking hours are Mon–Fri 8.30am–3pm. Some banks remain open later and at weekends to change money. There is also a 24-hour bureau de change at the airport. Beware that changing money can be outrageously expensive – banks either levy up to 12 percent in commission or charge a flat fee of around £15/US$20, regardless of the amount changed, so ask first. Automatic money-changing machines are much the easiest method of obtaining euros and they provide by far the best exchange rates.

Credit cards (*cartão de crédito*). Standard international credit cards are widely accepted in Madeira. However, in some shops and restaurants, especially in small villages, you may not be able to use a credit card.

Can I pay with this credit card?	**Posso pagar com cartão de crédito?**
I want to change some pounds/dollars.	**Queria trocar libras/dólares.**
Can you cash a traveller's cheque?	**Pode pagar um cheque de viagem?**
Where's the nearest bank/ currency exchange office?	**Onde fica o banco mais próximo/ a casa de câmbio mais próxima?**
How much is that?	**Quanto custa isto?**

ATMs (*caixa automática*). Automatic teller machines outside banks, identified by the MB (MultiBanco) sign, are widely available. From them you can draw funds in euros against your bank/credit card account with a Visa or Mastercard, or other debit card on one of the international networks such as Cirrus or Plus, provided you know the personal identification number (PIN). The PIN should be four digits.

Traveller's cheques. Less necessary now that ATMs have proliferated across the world, international traveller's cheques (such as those from Thomas Cook or American Express) can be cashed at any bank, although a high flat-rate fee is usually charged for changing them. Paying by traveller's cheque is invariably more expensive than paying by cash, due to the lower rate of exchange. Note that you will need to show your passport when using traveller's cheques.

OPENING HOURS *(horas de abertura)*

Though Madeirans do not take a siesta, most businesses close for a one- to two-hour lunch break. Shops and offices are generally open 9am–1pm and 3–7pm weekdays, and 9am–1pm Saturday. Banks are open 8.30am–3pm, Monday–Friday, while some also open Saturday 9am–1pm. Currency exchange offices generally open 9am–1pm and 2–7pm Monday–Saturday (closed Saturday afternoon).

Most museums open between 10am and 5pm weekdays; several close between 12.30 and 2pm, and most are closed on Monday and public holidays. Café-restaurants may be open all day, whereas more up-market establishments close after lunch and reopen for dinner.

Are you open?	**Está aberto?**
Are you closed?	**Está fechado?**

P

POLICE *(polícia)* (See also EMERGENCIES on page 113)

The national police, identified by their blue uniforms, are generally helpful and friendly and often speak a little English. If you need help or find yourself in an emergency situation, dial 112. The main

Where's the nearest police station?	**Onde fica o posto de polícia mais próximo?**
I've lost... my wallet/ bag/passport	**Perdi... a minha carteira/o meu saco/o meu passaporte**

police station in Funchal, where there is a lost property section, is on Rua João de Deus 7 (tel: 291 222022).

POST OFFICES *(correios)* (See also TELEPHONES on page 125)

Post offices are indicated by the letters CTT *(Correios, Telégrafos e Telefones)*. Mail boxes are painted bright red for second-class post and blue *(Correio Azul)* for first class (next-day delivery). Some post offices have separate slots for mail to the Portuguese mainland or international mail. The main post office in Funchal is on Avenida Zarco between Avenida Arriaga and Rua Carreira. It's open 8.30am–8pm Mon–Fri and 9.30am–1pm Sat. Local branches have shorter opening hours. You can buy stamps from tobacconists and kiosks, as well as at post offices.

A letter or postcard weighing up to 20g to EU countries costs €0.80; to the rest of the world, €1. Mail may take up to a week to reach a European destination.

Where's the nearest post office?	**Onde fica a estação de correios mais próxima?**
express (special delivery)	**expresso**
registered	**registrado**

PUBLIC TRANSPORT *(transporte público)*

Buses *(autocarro)*. Most of the island is covered by public buses, which are cheap, reliable and generally punctual. For those with the luxury of time and patience, it's possible to go almost anywhere that coach tours do by public bus – a much cheaper but more time-consuming alternative. The tourist office sells a booklet giving details of bus services and routes. Bus stops are indicated by the sign *paragem*.

The two largest bus operators are SAM and Rodoeste. They have their main departure points on the Avenida do Mar e das Comu-

Where is the nearest bus stop?	**Onde é a paragem de auto-carros mais próxima?**
When's the next bus to...?	**Quando parte o próximo autocarro para...?**
I want a ticket to... single/return	**Queria um bilhete para... ida/ida e volta**
Will you tell me when to get off?	**Pode dizer-me quando devo descer?**

nidades Madeirenses. You will find them between the Palácio de São Lourenço and the Zona Velha (Old Town).

Some intra-city and inter-city buses have identical bus numbers – for example, the orange town bus No 20 that goes to Monte is not the same as the green/cream island bus No 20 that travels to Santo da Serra.

Bus companies in Funchal have introduced a Giro card system which costs €0.50 to buy from automatic machines around the city or from authorised sellers. These cards are rechargeable, like the London Underground's Oyster cards, and need to be validated when you get on the bus. Various charges apply, depending on the number of zones travelled; the simplest and best deal is the €15 7-day pass. Children under 6 travel free and those aged 6–16 qualify for reduced fares.

Taxi. Metered taxis – which cannot be hailed in the street but are found at ranks all over Funchal and in every town – are reasonably priced and convenient for most trips within Funchal and to sights just outside the city (such as Monte, the Botanical Garden and the Quinta do Palheiro). For many popular tourist trips, there is a government-

Where can I get a taxi?	**Onde posso encontrar um táxi?**
What's the fare to...?	**Quanto custa um bilhete para...?**

set flat fare, which, by law, has to be displayed inside the taxi. Otherwise, the meter begins at €1.50. From the city centre to the hotel zone, expect to pay about €5. From the hotel zone to the airport costs between €20 and €30 depending on the time of day. All taxi rates are 20 percent higher after 10pm and at weekends and holidays.

Many people hire taxis as substitutes for coach tours to destinations around the island. If several people are travelling, this can be a good deal. (Most taxis will charge about €75 per half day or €150 for a full day.) A list of popular excursions and prices is kept at the tourist office.

Cable car. A cable car, which opened in 2000, connects Funchal's Zona Velha (Old Town) to Monte, in the mountains above the city. The trip takes approximately 15 minutes. Another cable car connects Monte to the Botanical Garden, and there are plans for several more to be built.

Flights to Porto Santo. Porto Santo can be easily reached several times a day by small aircraft from the airport in Madeira directly to Porto Santo's new airport. Flight time is approximately 15 minutes and costs about €75 return. Contract TAP, tel: 291 239211.

Ferry to Porto Santo. The Porto Santo Line (Rua da Praia 6; tel: 291 210300) operates a cruise-style ferry that departs from Funchal's harbour daily at 8am, arriving in Porto Santo about 2 hours later. It leaves Porto Santo at 6pm and costs around €36 return. (In winter the timetable is usually slightly reduced.) The new ships are far more stable than the old but travel pills are recommended for anyone prone to seasickness.

R

RELIGION

Madeira, like the rest of Portugal, is Roman Catholic. Catholic churches are found in every village, and visitors will find that patron saints' days are celebrated with religious rituals and festivities.

Anglican Sunday services are held in Funchal's English Church on Rua da Quebra Costas 18. The Scottish Kirk (Church), at the corner of Rua do Conselheiro and Rua Ivens, has services on the first Sunday of each month. There is also a Presbyterian church on Rua Consolado 47. The tourist information office has a list of services for English-speaking Catholics, and other services.

T

TELEPHONES *(telefone)*

Portugal's country code is 351. Within Madeira, the local area code, 291, must be dialled before all phone numbers, even for local calls (making nine digits in total).

Portugal Telecom public telephones that accept both coins and prepaid telephone cards are found all over Madeira. Coin boxes take a variety of euro coins; unused coins are returned. *Credifone* telephone cards, a better option, can be purchased at post offices or at newspaper kiosks. Local, national and international calls can also be made from hotels, but almost always with a substantial surcharge. You are wise to make these with an international calling card, if you must make them from your hotel room. Visitors from the US and Canada should be sure to get the international access code in Portugal for their long-distance telephone carrier at home.

To make a call, pick up the receiver, insert card or coin, wait for the dial tone, and dial. To make an international call, dial 00 for an international line + the country code (eg UK 0044, US 001) + phone number (including the area code, without the initial '0'

Can you get me this number?	**Pode ligar-me para este número?**
reverse-charge (collect) call	**paga pelo destinatário**
person-to-person (personal) call	**com pré-aviso**

where there is one). If you wish to send a fax, you may do so from most hotels, though the charge may seem high.

Dial 099 for the international operator for Europe, and 098 for the rest of the world. For directory enquiries within Madeira, telephone 118.

TIME DIFFERENCES *(hora local)*

Madeira operates both winter (GMT + 0) and summer (GMT + 1) time periods. If you are travelling from Britain, do not adjust your watch, as Madeira is on the same time. From the last Sunday in March until the last Sunday in October, the clocks are moved one hour ahead for summer time.

Summer time chart

Sydney	Madeira	London	Los Angeles	New York
9pm	noon	noon	4am	7am

TIPPING *(serviço; gorjeta)*

Hotel and restaurant bills are generally all-inclusive, but an additional tip of 5–10 percent is common and even expected in restaurants. Hotel wages are not high, and tips help to boost the income of staff: porters generally receive €1 per bag, the maid who cleans your room €1 per day. Taxi drivers do not normally expect a tip, though one should be given for any special services or information rendered.

TOILETS *(toilete; lavabo; quarto de banho; serviços)*

Public toilets in Funchal are few and far between, and not usually recommended. The best place to find a clean toilet is in a large hotel

Where are the toilets please?	¿Por favor, onde é o lavabo/ quarto de banho?

or a restaurant or bar. (In the latter, out of courtesy you should buy a drink, or at least ask permission.) 'Ladies' is marked *Senhoras* and 'Gents' *Homens* or *Senhores*. Be careful not to confuse *Senhoras* and *Senhores*.

TOURIST INFORMATION *(oficina de turismo; informação turística)*

Portugal does not have national tourist offices as such. Instead it maintains a website – Visit Portugal (<www.visitportugal.com>) – from which various brochures can be ordered. In addition, Madeira has its own website – Madeira Tourism (<www.madeiratourism. com>) – with plenty of information on the destination. If none of these sources is able to answer your questions, you could try contacting the following offices of ICEP *(Investimentos, Comércio e Turismo de Portugal)*.

Canada: Suite 1005, 60 Bloor Street West, Toronto, Ontario M4W 3B8; tel: 416-921 7376.

Ireland: 54 Dawson Street, Dublin 2; tel: 01-670 9133.

South Africa: 5th Floor, Mercantile Lisbon House, 142 West Street, Sandown 2196, Johannesburg; tel: 2711-302 0404.

UK: Portuguese Embassy, 11 Belgrave Square, London SW1X 8PP; tel: 020-7201 6666; brochure line: 0845 355 1212; email: <tourism @portugaloffice.org.uk>.

US: 590 Fifth Ave, 4th floor, New York, NY10036; tel: 646-723 0200.

The Regional Department of Tourism in Madeira has 10 offices. The tourist information office in Funchal, the most dependable (tel: 291 211900; email: <info@madeiratourism.com>), is at Avenida Arriaga 18. It's open Mon–Fri 9am–8pm; Sat–Sun 9am–6pm. The airport tourist office (tel: 291 524933) is open daily 9am–8pm. Provincial offices in Caniço, Machico, Ribeira Brava, Câmara de Lobos, Porto Moniz, Santana and Porto Santo keep normal business hours, though most close for lunch and a couple are not open in the afternoon.

WEBSITES AND INTERNET CAFÉS

www.madeira-island.com A periodic webzine with events, chat room and links to travel providers, hotels etc.

www.madeira-web.com Run by a commercial travel agent, in English, German, Spanish and Portuguese, with a guide to outdoor activities, island tours and property.

www.madeiraonline.com A web portal with links to bargain flights to Madeira, lists of doctors and health services, the performing arts, sports and more, mostly in English.

www.madeiratourism.org A helpful site with lots of up-to-date travel information, published by the Madeira Board of Tourism.

www.madeiraapartments.com A guide to self-catering accommodation on Madeira as an alternative to hotels.

www.madeirawine.com Information on local wines and an e-shop.

Internet Cafés

Cybercafe (Avenida do Infante 6) charges a variable rate for computer use and Internet connection. Alternatively try **Cremesoda. com**, at Rua dos Ferreiros 9, (tel: 291 224920), which offers Internet access and email services.

WEIGHTS AND MEASURES

Like most of Europe, Portugal uses the metric system.

YOUTH HOSTELS *(Centros de Juventude)*

There are three official youth hostels in Madeira (in Funchal, Calheta and Porto Moniz) and one on Porto Santo. See the website of the International Youth Hostelling Federation at <www.hihostels. com> for further information.

Recommended Hotels

Madeira's hotels, many of them offering traditional, older style accommodation, have long been clustered in the hotel and tourist zones hugging the coast west of Funchal. In recent years, many of these hotels have been urgently updating their design and services, as even more hotels are being built in the *zona turista*. At the same time, hotel accommodation across the island is rapidly being expanded, and visitors can now choose from hotels, *quintas* (villas), *estalagens* and *pousadas* (inns) along the coast and in the villages and mountains of the interior.

Book especially early for Christmas and New Year (when most hotels charge a huge supplement) and for smaller hotels throughout the year. Otherwise, high season rates generally apply from Easter through May and July to the end of September. Price guidelines below are for a double room with bath in high season, including breakfast and VAT (value-added tax). All hotels accept major credit cards. For making reservations, Portugal's country code is 351; the area code for Madeira is 291.

€€€€	over 200 euros
€€€	150–200 euros
€€	100–150 euros
€	below 100 euros

FUNCHAL INNER HOTEL ZONE

Aparthotel Imperatriz € *Rua da Imperatriz Dona Amélia 72, 9000 Funchal; tel: 233456; fax: 229558; <www.hotel-imperatriz. pt>*. Surrounded by luxury hotels, and adjacent to the Casino, these studio apartments, all with kitchenette and balcony, have a rooftop swimming pool with views of the sea. A good choice for those on a tight budget. 27 studios.

Avenue Park Apartamentos Turísticos €€ *Avenida do Infante 26, 9000 Funchal; tel: 205630; fax: 205659; <www.avenuepark-madeira.com>*. Smart, modern apartments (studios and one- and two-bedroom apartments) located across from the Santa Catarina Park and the Casino, and no more than a five-minute walk from Funchal's city centre. Fashionably equipped with modern furnishings in bright colours and nice, clean kitchenettes. Disabled access. 15 apartments.

Cliff Bay Hotel €€€€ *Estrada Monumental 147, 9000 Funchal; tel: 707700, freephone in UK: 0800-964328; fax: 762 5245; <www.cliffbay.com>.* Luxurious hotel set on a clifftop opposite the Lido supermarket, with panoramic sea and harbour views from nearly all its rooms. Guests are pampered with large, fashionable rooms, and spacious and well-equipped bathrooms. Facilities include two pools (one of them a seawater lagoon), a health club, tennis court, three restaurants and four bars. Disabled access. 201 rooms.

Madeira Regency Club €€€ *Rua Carvalho Araújo 9, 9000 Funchal; tel: 205757; fax: 205733; <www.regency-hotels-resorts.com>.* Spacious and well-equipped poolside apartments with sun terraces and access to the sea. Heated seawater pool and children's pool. Most rooms overlook the sea and harbour. The staff are exceptionally friendly. Other facilities include a sauna and squash courts. Disabled access. 96 rooms.

Penha de França €–€€ *Rua da Imperatriz Dona Amélia 85, 9000 Funchal; tel: 775936; fax: 762171; <www.penhafranca.com>.* Restored manor house *(albergaria)* tucked away in a lovely garden in the midst of Funchal's hotel district. Although small and intimate, it nevertheless has a piano bar, outdoor dining, a lawn and pool with an expansive terrace and terrific sea views. Stylish rooms. Disabled access. 76 rooms.

Pestana Carlton Madeira €€€€ *Largo António Nobre, 9000 Funchal; tel: 239500; fax: 223377; <www.pestana.com>.* Attractive, luxurious 5-star complex sitting on a clifftop overlooking Funchal Bay. The hotel spans a river gorge with direct views of the sea. The rooms are large and comfortable, and all have balconies. Four restaurants and lively nightlife, as well as tennis court, two swimming pools, diving school and other sports facilities. Package deals are available. Disabled access. 375 rooms.

Pestana Casino Park €€€€ *Rua da Imperatriz Dona Amélia 55, 9000 Funchal; tel: 209100; fax: 232076; <www.pestana.com>.* Large 1960s concrete complex (designed by Brazilian architect Oscar Niemeyer) set within its own gardens overlooking the coast and Funchal's harbour. It takes the resort part of its name seriously, with a large swimming pool, activities and nightly entertainment at the adjacent casino and nightclubs. The tastefully furnished rooms all have balconies. Given a total refurbishment in 2006, this is still slightly less expensive than competing 5-star hotels. Disabled access. 327 rooms.

Quinta Perestrello €€€ *Rua Dr. Pita 3, 9000 Funchal; tel: 775936; fax: 762171; <www.quintaperestrellomadeira.com>.* Delightful 150-year-old country house with period antiques, a lovely garden and swimming pool. Located close to Quinta do Magnolia park, but adjacent to a busy road junction, so some rooms can be subject to traffic noise. The restaurant serves light meals, but guests can use all the facilities at sister hotels in the Charming Hotels Madeira group. 36 rooms.

Reid's Palace €€€€ *Estrada Monumental 139, 9000 Funchal; tel: 717171 (in US and Canada tel: 800 237 1236 (toll-free); in UK tel: 0845 077 2222 (local call rate); fax: 717177; <www.reidspalace. com>.* Madeira's legendary hotel is a magnificent mansion that preserves the elegance of another era. Sumptuously redecorated in 2006, the hotel has magnificent gardens overlooking the sea, spacious sun terraces, pools and tennis courts. Wide variety of packages, some of which are surprisingly affordable at certain times of the year. Disabled access. 173 rooms.

Savoy Resort €€€€ *Avenida do Infante, 9004 Funchal; tel: 213000; fax: 223103; <www.savoyresort.com>.* Two great hotels under one management – the traditional Classic Savoy (337 rooms) has an unprepossessing exterior that belies the opulence of its public rooms, while the Royal Savoy (162 rooms) has an unrivalled pool and sports complex. If you can't decide which to go for, the older Classic is slightly cheaper, and guests have full use of the Royal's beautifully landscaped seafront lido; it is slightly old-fashioned (in the best possible sense) compared to the Royal Hotel, with its African and Asian antiques and tribal rugs and its modern room decor. Both have excellent restaurants: a fine top-floor grill room in the Classic and a fusion-food restaurant in the Royal. Disabled access. 350 rooms.

FUNCHAL TOURIST ZONE

Crowne Plaza Resort Madeira €€€€ *Estrada Monumental 175–7, 9000 Funchal; tel: 717700; fax: 717701; <www.crowneplaza.com>.* The Crowne Plaza is formed by twin towers separated by a low block with a wave-shaped roof. The Philippe Starck-designed décor is minimalist and stylish, and all rooms have panoramic sea views. Four restaurants, an Irish pub, two indoor and two outdoor pools, spa, tennis and squash courts, and a diving centre. Disabled access. 300 rooms.

Eden Mar Suite Hotel €€€ *Rua do Gorgulho 2, 9004 Funchal; tel: 709700; fax: 761966; <www.edenmar.com>.* A well-equipped, popular, and modern aparthotel set in a busy location in the heart of the tourist zone. Part of the Eden Mar shopping complex, with shops, bars and restaurants on the doorstep. All studios have kitchenette, private balcony and sea views. Guests have access to outdoor and indoor pools set in lush gardens, squash, snooker, health club and sauna, sun terrace with a pleasant garden, and restaurant. Disabled access. 146 rooms.

Hotel Girassol €€€ *Estrada Monumental 256, 9004 Funchal; tel: 701570; fax: 765441; email: <hotelgirassol@mail.telepac.pt>.* A modern hotel, pleasant and friendly, with a consistent package business. Rooms are basic, but each has a terrace or balcony overlooking the garden, the mountains or the sea. Despite being located on the busy main Funchal highway, the hotel has a secluded garden and swimming pool. It also has a restaurant, which has sea views and, at dinner, live music. Disabled access. 133 rooms.

Madeira Palácio €€€ *Estrada Monumental, 265, 9000 Funchal; tel: 702702; fax: 702703; <www.hotelmadeirapalacio.com>*. One of the old-time favourites in Madeira, this traditional hotel is struggling to keep pace with its 5-star neighbours, but it has attractive grounds, good views, tennis courts and a nice swimming pool. Recent renovation of the lobby, giving it a colonial appearance, and the addition of an indoor pool are very welcome. Disabled access. 253 rooms.

Pensão Vila Vicência € *Rua da Casa Branca 45, 9000 Funchal; tel: 771527; fax: 771538; email: <vicencia@mail.telepac.pt>*. A delightful, family-run pension comprising three adjacent houses, Vila Vicência is just a five-minute walk from the Lido complex. It has a lovely small garden with a private swimming pool. 30 rooms.

Pestana Palms €€€ *Rua do Gorgulho 17, 9000 Funchal; tel: 709200; fax: 766247; <www.pestana.com>*. This aparthotel on the seafront incorporates a refurbished *quinta*. All rooms are nicely furnished, self-catering studios. Heated pool, health club, gymnasium and special touches including a diving club and school, and free Internet use. 167 rooms.

Pestana Village €€€ *Estrada Monumental 194, 9000 Funchal; tel: 701600; fax: 765727; <www.pestana.com>*. Looking like a well-designed village straight out of a Mexican resort, the Village Aparthotel has a faux-Moorish lobby and a beautifully landscaped swimming pool area and gardens. Nicely equipped studio apartment suites and a relaxing spa centre. Half-board available. Disabled access. 200 rooms.

Tivoli Ocean Park Resort Hotel €€€€ *Rua Simplício dos Passos Gouveia 29, 9004 Funchal; tel: 702000; fax: 702020; <www.tivolihotels.com>*. Another of the big and bold 5-star hotels to sprout along the coast in the tourist zone, the Tivoli Ocean Park competes with the Crowne Plaza to see which offers more of everything. It is awash with sports, facilities and services, and the modern rooms, which all have balconies and sea views, are plush. Disabled access. 349 rooms.

Castanheiro € *Rua do Castanheiro 27, 9000 Funchal; tel: 227060; fax: 227940.* Good-value apartments in an excellent location just off Praça do Município. Well-equipped rooms and friendly staff. The adjacent snack-bar restaurant is recommended. 32 apartments.

Porto Santa Maria €€€ *Avenida do Mar e das Comunidades Madeirenses 50, 9050 Funchal; tel: 206700; fax: 206727; <www. portostamaria.com>.* On the seafront in the Old Town, next to the 17th-century São Tiago fortress. Rooms are modern, and studio apartments are also available. Disabled access. 147 rooms.

Quinta da Bela Vista €€€€ *Caminho do Avista Navios 4, 9000 Funchal; tel: 706400; fax: 706401; <www.belavistamadeira.com>.* A plush hotel at the eastern end of the Old Town, built around an elegant 19th-century mansion, with splendid views and a lovely garden. The beautiful rooms are furnished with antiques. Excellent food at the formal restaurant. Small gym and sauna, swimming pool, library. 67 rooms.

Santa Maria € *Rua João de Deus 26, 9050 Funchal; tel: 225271; fax: 221542.* Simple hotel in the Old Town, very close to some excellent restaurants. Rooftop swimming pool with views of all Funchal. 83 rooms.

Windsor €€ *Rua das Hortas 4, 9050 Funchal; tel: 233081; fax: 233080; <www.hotelwindsorgroup.pt>.* Modern hotel right in the busy centre of Funchal. Rather plain rooms without views, but good facilities and service, and a very nice rooftop pool and terrace. Both convenient and reasonably priced. Disabled access. 67 rooms.

Casa das Videiras € *Sítio Serra d'Água, 9270 Seixal; tel: 854020; fax: 222667; <www.casa-das-videiras.com>.* Charming guesthouse in a tiny, pretty town on the north coast. The mid-19th-century manor house has clean and attractively decorated rooms, and the atmosphere is very friendly and relaxed – a tribute to the hands-on owner. Self-catering possible. Deals available: seven nights for the price of six, 14 nights for 12. 4 rooms.

Casa do Caseiro € *Caminho do Monte 62, 9050 Funchal; tel: 740550; fax: 227113; <www.casadocaseiro.com>*. High above Funchal, halfway down Monte's famous toboggan run. Small, charming, private house, attractive gardens, pool and terrace with lovely views. 7 rooms.

Casa Velha do Palheiro €€€€ *Rua da Estalagem 23, São Gonçalo, 9060 Funchal; tel: 790350; fax: 794925; <www.casa-velha. com>*. Nestled in the hills east of Funchal, with great views of the city, this handsome and stylish inn occupies a beautiful 1804 country-estate house connected to the Palheiro Gardens. Luxuriously decorated rooms. Part of the esteemed Palheiro Golf Club (special golf packages available) – the only hotel in Madeira on a golf course – and with an elegant restaurant, heated pool, gym and tennis court. 37 rooms.

Choupana Hills Resort €€€€ *Travessa do Largo da Choupana, 9060 Funchal; tel: 206020; fax: 206021; <www.choupanahills. com>*. One of a new generation of hotels on Madeira catering for international jet-setting clients, the Choupana Hills combines Balinese-style timber bungalows with all mod cons, and lush subtropical gardens watered by a typical Madeiran *levada*, which you can follow westwards to Monte or eastwards to the Palheiro Gardens. Alternatively, laze in the hotel's large and well-equipped spa, and enjoy casual all-day dining on local specialities or 'fusion' food in the excellent Xôpana restaurant. 60 rooms.

Dom Pedro Baía €€–€€€ *Estrada de São Roque, 9200 Machico; tel: 775936; fax: 762171; <www.dompedrobaiahotel.com>*. A modern high-rise overlooking the bay of Machico, this comfortable hotel is a good base for exploring the eastern part of the island. Popular with British and German package tours, it has an Olympic-size swimming pool, tennis court, bar and nightly entertainment. Disabled access. 218 rooms.

Estalagem da Ponta do Sol €€ *Quinta da Rochinha, 9360 Ponta do Sol; tel: 970200; fax: 970209; <www.pontadosol.com>*. Another modern boutique hotel that undermines the image of Madeira as a resort for the retired, the Ponta do Sol is a Modernist dream, consisting of a series of white-walled cubes with plate-glass windows set on the clifftop east of Ponta do Sol village. The delightful gardens and bar are set in the original mansion, while the excellent restaurant is perfectly positioned for glorious views of the sunset. 54 rooms.

Estalagem do Mar € *Sítio dos Juncos, Fajã da Areia, 9240 São Vicente; tel: 840010; fax: 840019; <www.hotelestalagemdomar>*. Within walking distance of São Vicente, and sandwiched between a sheer cliff and the roaring sea, this sprawling hotel buys exclusivity at a bargain price. All the rooms, which are simply furnished, face the ocean. Indoor and outdoor pool, restaurant and tennis court. 99 rooms.

Estalagem Eira do Serrado €€–€€€ *Eira do Serrado, Curral das Freiras, 9000 Funchal; tel: 710060; fax: 710061; <www.eirado serrado.com>*. This 4-star guesthouse with elegant rooms, all with balconies, occupies a splendid setting right on the rim of the hidden valley of Curral das Freiras. Enchanting views are guaranteed as you look down over green terraces to the isolated village in the valley far below, or up to the jagged volcanic peaks that encircle the skyline. Games room, restaurant, Jacuzzi, sauna and wine cellar. 25 rooms.

Estalagem Quinta do Estreito €€€€ *Rua José Joaquim da Costa, 9325 Estreito de Câmara de Lobos; tel: 775936; fax: 910549; <www.quintadoestreito.com>*. A luxury *quinta*, or villa, with elegant furnishings set 400m (1,300ft) above sea level, overlooking the vineyards of Câmara de Lobos. A relaxing hideaway, the *quinta* has landscaped tropical gardens, restaurant, library and heated pool. Comfortable, tastefully decorated rooms. 48 rooms.

Pousada dos Vinháticos €€ *Fajã dos Vinháticos, Serra d'Água, 9350 Ribeira Brava; tel: 952344; fax: 952540; <www.dorisol.pt>*. This chalet-style inn – owned by the Dorisol hotel group, not by the

Portuguese government as *pousadas* are on the mainland – is a terrific mountain refuge, ideal for nature enthusiasts and those in search of serenity. The inn is set in a splendid wood-cabin lodge (imported from Finland) with unmatched views and comfortable rooms. Good-value restaurant, games room and very friendly, knowledgeable staff. 21 rooms.

Quinta do Furão €€ *Achada do Gramacho, 9230 Santana; tel: 570100; fax: 573560; <www.quintadofurao.com>.* Newly built in rustic stlye, this rural inn is set amidst a sea of green orchards and grapevines, with views of the undulating hills around Santana. The best hotel in the area, the 'Quinta of the Otter' offers style and relaxation, with a cool little pool with a retractable roof, and a fine rustic restaurant. 43 rooms.

Residencial Amparo € *Rua da Amargura, 9200 Machico; tel: 968120; fax: 960050; <www.residencialamparo.web.pt>.* A simple hotel, comfortably decorated, in the centre of Machico, just two blocks from the seafront. A pleasant and personal alternative to the larger and more institutional Dom Pedro. Attractive restaurant. 12 rooms.

Residencial Encumeada € *Feiteiras, Serra d'Água, 9350 Ribeira Brava; tel: 951281; fax: 951281; <www.residencialencumeada. com>.* Few places can match the setting of this unpretentious lodging. Just down the road from the Encumeada pass, the hotel sits on a ledge overlooking the mountains and valley around Serra de Água, half-way between the north and south coasts. Absolutely ideal for walkers and hikers. 50 rooms.

PORTO SANTO

Torre Praia €€€ *Rua Goulart Medeiros, 9400 Porto Santo; tel: 980450; fax: 982487; <www.torrepraia.pt>.* Just outside Vila Baleira, this attractive 4-star hotel has simple furnishings and overlooks Porto Santo's excellent beach and the ocean. Kidney-shaped swimming pool, squash court, gym, sauna and Jacuzzi, games room and three restaurants. 65 rooms.

Recommended Restaurants

For most visitors dining in Madeira used to be limited to hotels and the odd café or snack bar encountered in Funchal or wherever their coach stopped for lunch during an all-day tour. But the restaurant scene is improving and catering for a more diverse clientele, and while some of the finest restaurants on the island are still found in the top hotels, there is now a wider variety than ever.

Restaurants known as *típicos* are basic eateries (often rustic, or at least decorated in a rustic style), where the menu is often limited to Madeiran dishes *(pratos típicos)*. A good *típico* is worth a detour, but some of them have been spoiled by a constant stream of coach and cruise passengers; they seem more intent on separating tourists from their euros than offering genuine Madeiran food.

The prices indicated are for starter, main course and dessert, with wine, per person. (Note that some fish or shellfish dishes will be more expensive.) Service and VAT of 16 percent are included, as they generally are in the bill, but it is customary to leave an additional 5–10 percent tip for good service. Except where noted, all restaurants accept major credit cards.

When making reservations, remember that all telephone numbers must be prefaced by the area code, 291.

€€€€	over 40 euros
€€€	25–40 euros
€€	15–25 euros
€	less than 15 euros

FUNCHAL TOWN

Golden Gate Grand Café €–€€ *Avenida Arriaga 29; tel: 234383*. Open daily for lunch and dinner. This café, in a 19th-century house on the main street, is a great spot for people-watching. Choose from a light menu downstairs, or a full menu upstairs in the restaurant.

O Celeiro €€–€€€ *Rua dos Aranhas 22; tel: 230622*. Open daily for lunch and dinner. This highly rated rustic cellar is popular with both locals and foreign visitors. Fresh fish, *espetadas* (kebabs) and *cataplana* are among the house specialities. Good wine list.

Restaurant Caravela €€€ *Avenida das Comunidades Madeirenses 15 (3rd floor); tel: 225471.* Open Mon–Sat for lunch and dinner. This 30-year-old city-centre restaurant is popular for its panoramic ocean views and Portuguese cuisine focusing on fresh fish and shellfish. There's a glass-enclosed terrace as well as an inner dining room.

FUNCHAL HOTEL ZONE

Casa dos Reis €€€ *Rua Imperatriz Dona Amélia 101; tel: 225182.* Open daily for dinner. An attractive and small, formal restaurant, serving a wide range of international, French and Portuguese dishes. Try the charcoal-grilled lamb or scabbard fish, an island speciality, with green pepper sauce.

Casa Velha €€€ *Rua Imperatriz Dona Amélia 69; tel: 205600.* Open daily for lunch and dinner. A formal garden-like restaurant with bamboo chairs, ferns and ceiling fans, the 'Old House' has a 19th-century colonial feel. The short international and Madeiran menu is popular with nearby hotel guests. Piano bar downstairs.

Dona Amélia €€–€€€ *Rua Imperatriz Dona Amélia 83; tel: 225784.* Open daily for lunch and dinner. This chic upstairs restaurant behind the Savoy Hotel is a good place for a romantic dinner of *espetadas* (kebabs), grilled fish, nice salads and soups.

Fleur de Lys €€€€ *Avenida do Infante (in Savoy Hotel); tel: 213000.* Open daily for dinner. The Savoy Hotel's entry in the luxury dining category is outstanding. Located on the hotel's eighth floor, it has spectacular panoramic views, as well as old-world elegance and service. The French menu, overseen by a Michelin-starred chef, is meticulously prepared and presented.

Joe's Bar €–€€ *Rua da Penha de França; tel: 229087.* Open daily for lunch and dinner. Eat on the lovely garden terraces or in an attractive dining room. Check out the blackboard menu outside, which includes a dish of the day, often a fresh fish course.

Kon Tiki €€ *Rua do Favila 9; tel: 764737.* Open daily for lunch and dinner. Offering an interesting menu of Madeiran favourites with an international twist, such as shark steak and *espada* with prawns flambé, as well as specialities from Finland (fillet steak prepared on a hot stone).

Les Faunes €€€€ *Estrada Monumental 139 (in Reid's Palace Hotel); tel: 717030.* Open daily for dinner. (In summer, Les Faunes moves out onto the hotel's open-air terrace and becomes the Brisa Mar restaurant.) Reid's elegant winter restaurant is something special. The standard-bearer on Madeira for French-style haute cuisine, the elegant dining room overlooking the harbour is the place for refined atmosphere, with piano accompaniment.

Quinta do Palmeira €€€–€€€€ *Avenida do Infante 5; tel: 221814.* Open daily for lunch and dinner. One of Madeira's finest restaurants, this handsome 18th-century townhouse has an elegantly appointed dining room and a terrace for open-air dining. Many terrific dishes, including smoked swordfish wrapped round hearts of palm and served with caviar, and *espada* with bananas and passion-fruit sauce. Excellent wine list and attentive service.

FUNCHAL TOURIST ZONE

Casa Madeirense €€€ *Estrada Monumental 153; tel: 766700.* Open Mon–Sat for lunch and dinner. In the midst of the tourist zone's biggest 5-star hotels, this comfortable restaurant nearly goes overboard with regional gastronomy and folklore (the bar looks like a *palheiro*, the typical A-frame house of Santana). However, it's a popular place, good for *cataplana de mariscos* and other seafood.

O Tokos €€€ *Estrada Monumental 169; tel: 771019.* Open Tues–Sun for lunch and dinner. A tiny restaurant with an eccentric chef/owner, this intimate place (just 10 or so tables) does everything well, but when the chef (Felipe dos Ramos) wheels out the trolley of fresh fish, you'll be hard-pressed to order anything else. Fresh vegetables, excellent desserts and a very good wine cellar. Reservations essential.

Tropical €€€ *Estrada Monumental 306 (in Hotel Florasol); tel: 700840.* Open daily. One of Funchal's most popular restaurants, with an international/Madeiran menu famous for its *flambé* desserts. Live music and a boisterous crowd nightly.

Villa Cipriani €€€ *Estrada Monumental 139; tel: 717171.* Open daily for dinner. Just down the road from Reid's Palace, this handsome Italian restaurant (owned by Reid's) serves excellent pastas, fish and meat dishes, complemented by a terrific wine list. Have a cocktail at the bar and wait for a table on the terrace.

BEYOND FUNCHAL

Casa Velha do Palheiro €€€€ *Palheiro Golf, São Gonçalo; tel: 790350.* Open daily for lunch and dinner. The refined dining room in the grounds of the Quinta do Palheiro hotel is one of the island's most elegant restaurants. Exquisite French and Portuguese dishes. Daily fixed-price and à la carte menu. Superb service and wine list.

Estalagem do Mar € *Sítio dos Juncos, Fajã da Areia, São Vicente; tel: 840010.* Open daily for lunch and dinner. A popular hotel restaurant with panoramic views of the ocean. Both hotel guests and visitors can be assured of a dependable, reasonably priced meal of fresh seafood, including swordfish and sea bass.

O Cachalote €€ *Ilhéumar, Porto Moniz; tel: 291853.* Open daily for lunch. Perched on the rocks overlooking the natural pools of Porto Moniz, this restaurant is renowned for its Madeiran specialities and well-prepared seafood dishes. Stupendous panoramic ocean views from two floors.

Pousada dos Vinháticos €€–€€€ *Fajã dos Vinháticos, Serra d'Água; tel: 952344.* Open daily for lunch and dinner. This chalet-style inn has an excellent restaurant with panoramic views of the surrounding mountains. It serves mostly Madeiran and Portuguese specialities, but does an excellent chateaubriand for two. Nice wine list and friendly service. Downstairs bar and outdoor terrace.

Praça do Engeno €€ *Rua da Praia, Porto da Cruz;* tel: 560080. Open daily lunch and dinner. The *engeno* of this restaurant's name refers to the location on the seafront at Porta da Cruz inside the converted engine room of a former sugar mill. Grey basalt walls lit by modern plate glass provide the setting for a leisurely meal of fresh seafood which you can choose for yourself from a selection laid out on a bed of ice.

Quinta do Arco Tea Rooms € *Quinta do Arco, Sítio da Lagoa, Arco de São Jorge; tel: 570270.* Open Tues–Sun 10am–7pm, closed Jan–April. This is a great place to stop and stretch your legs on a tour of Madeira's north coast because as well as an extensive choice of teas with homemade bread, cakes, scones and jam, plus a full menu of good home-made food, you can wander around an extensive rose garden packed with 130 different varieties of rose.

Quinta do Furão €€ *Achada do Gramacho, Santana;* tel: 570100. Open daily for lunch and dinner. This rustic restaurant, part of the hotel of the same name, serves some of the finest food on the entire north coast. Surrounded by orchards and a vineyard, it offers the freshest of local ingredients and seafood.

Victor's Bar €€ *Ribeiro Frio; tel: 575898.* Open daily lunch and dinner. A cosy bar reminiscent of an English pub leads to a chalet-like dining area with a fireplace. Grilled trout, plucked fresh from the hatchery across the road, is the house speciality.

PORTO SANTO

Teodorico € *Serra do Dentro; tel: 982257.* Open daily lunch and dinner. This comfortable, former farmhouse, popular with locals and visitors, is the place in Porto Santo to get *espetada* – grilled beef served on a skewer. Nearly everyone orders the *espetada*, which is served with vegetables, potatoes and excellent Madeiran bread, *pão de caco*. Outdoor seating. No credit cards.

INDEX

pocket guide

Madeira

Fourth Edition 2008

Written by Neil Schlecht
Updated by Christopher Catling
Series Editor: Tony Halliday

All Rights Reserved
© 2008 Berlitz Publishing/Apa Publications GmbH & Co. Verlag KG, Singapore Branch, Singapore

Printed in Singapore by Insight Print Services (Pte) Ltd, 38 Joo Koon Road, Singapore 628990. Tel: (65) 6865-1600. Fax: (65) 6861-6438

Berlitz Trademark Reg. U.S. Patent Office and other countries. Marca Registrada

Photography credits
Chris Coe/Apa 15; Glyn Genin/Apa 6, 44, 59, 64, 66, 69, 90, 93; Paul Murphy/Apa 30; Neil Schlecht/Apa 8, 10, 11, 27, 28, 31, 38, 40, 42, 45, 50, 53, 56, 76; Phil Wood/Apa 1, 13, 16, 21, 24, 43, 47, 61, 62, 63, 67, 72, 73, 74, 80, 94, 96, 98; Berlitz 51, 65; Madeira Tourism 26, 33, 34, 37, 42, 48, 49, 54, 60, 70, 79, 82, 84, 87, 88, 89; Mary Evans Picture Library 18, 22

Cover picture: Pictures Colour Library/Clive Sawyer

Every effort has been made to provide accurate information in this publication, but changes are inevitable. The publisher cannot be responsible for any resulting loss, inconvenience or injury.

Contact us

At Berlitz we strive to keep our guides as accurate and up to date as possible, but if you find anything that has changed, or if you have any suggestions on ways to improve this guide, then we would be delighted to hear from you.

Berlitz Publishing, PO Box 7910, London SE1 1WE, England.
fax: (44) 20 7403 0290
email: berlitz@apaguide.co.uk
www.berlitzpublishing.com